Doing Up Old Junk

Doing Up Old Junk

JOANNA JONES

BCA

LONDON   NEW YORK   SYDNEY   TORONTO

This edition published 1995 by BCA by arrangement
with Merehurst Limited, Ferry House
51–57 Lacy Road, Putney, London SW15 1PR

Reprinted 1996

A catalogue record of this book is available from the
British Library.

Edited by Heather Dewhurst
Designed by Rita Wüthrich
Photography by Jon Bouchier
Styling by Joanna Jones
Illustration by King & King

Typeset by Servis Filmsetting Ltd, Manchester
Colour separation by Global Colour, Malaysia
Printed in Italy by New Interlitho

**To the Guv, the best bit of old junk
I've ever found!**

Acknowledgements
I would like to thank my dear friend Marjorie Smith for storing all the furniture for the book in her garage over Christmas so that my family could get into the dining room to eat.

I would also like to thank John Payne for his heroic efforts in transporting the furniture for photography, which certainly went beyond the call of duty.

Contents

Introduction

Although the majority of this book is about the equipment and techniques needed to do up old junk, I feel that I would be failing in my duty if I didn't also give you a thorough grounding in the equipment and techniques needed to acquire it in the first place.

Any good junk collector worth his or her salt will have a regular routine of actually seeking out junk and will not only have a list of favourite and fruitful venues, but will also scan the newspapers, notice boards and even lamp posts for further signs of activity.

Even so, much of the junk you find you will come upon quite accidentally and more often than not for free or, at any rate, for very little.

Free (or Almost Free) Junk

At the beginning of your career at least, you will have recourse to a sizeable collection of home-grown junk. Check your own loft and garage and those of your friends and family, before opening up dealings with total strangers.

When you have exhausted the home market the time will have come to make overtures to the 'in house' refuse collectors at the municipal tip. These are the people who oversee the dumping of all domestic rubbish and quite often the abandoning of extremely useable junk. Luckily, many ordinary citizens fail to make the distinction between the two and actually drive wonderful

▶ **The dining room**
All the furniture in this dining room is oak and would have looked dark and heavy if still covered with its original varnish. As it is, the stripping and colourwashing have lifted the tone without losing the effect of the oak grain.

pieces of furniture to their fate themselves.

Unfortunately, if you do spot just what you are looking for, or even something you didn't *know* you were looking for, at the tip . . . money invariably has to change hands. To be fair it usually isn't very much money and the guardians of the tip deserve something for separating the Chippendale from the potato peelings.

People also throw rubbish into skips which they hire and leave outside their houses in the road. Nine times out of ten these contain splintered wood, rubble, smelly carpets and what appears to be a statutory mattress. Occasionally, though, interesting pieces of furniture will be tossed out of the house and this is when you knock smartly on the door and ask if you can remove it. The owners are usually so glad to have extra space in their skip that they will give you the item gladly, and even help you into the car with it! By the way, removing prize items from skips in the dead of night is considered bad form and is probably illegal!

Flea Markets & Junk Collector's Fairs

You will notice at your first flea market or junk collector's fair that there is a strange lack of animation on the faces of both the vendors and the buyers, but particularly the latter. This is something which you must develop if you wish to become a successful junk collector, that is one who does not pay over the odds.

It is very difficult to evince total disinterest in an object especially if you have been tracking down just such a thing for weeks, but for almost every type of bargain hunting/junk collecting, it does become necessary to develop an air of studied boredom with the whole business. Poker players and orientals who have an innate talent for such desirable inscrutability make formidable bargain hunters, but for the rest of us I am afraid it is just practice, practice and even more practice.

Learn to sidle up to things (never run) and while you are examining it for woodworm, rust, etc, look seriously concerned, even if the object is in pristine condition. Frown a lot and try any working parts it may have with a look of confusion, as if something vital is missing.

Discuss the object in whispers with your friend or partner and even if you are *actually* saying 'My God, I've found it at last! Isn't it perfect!', shake your head repeatedly and look extremely doubtful.

If there are no obvious contenders around, you could even go so far as to put the object down and take a few steps away.

If the seller is as well versed in the ritual as you are and has so far said nothing, you may then have to drift back and enquire languidly after the price.

An experienced vendor will then give you the item's life history, and maybe even their own as well, rather than come right out with such a piece of valuable information. However, after a few more frowns from you and maybe even a glance at your watch, the price will eventually be mentioned. Be prepared for it, because at this point you must draw in your breath sharply and look at first mockingly and then in utter disbelief at both the object and the vendor.

After that it is in the lap of the gods. You will state what you think it's worth and how much work needs doing to it, etc. The vendor will point out its rarity value and the multitude of other people who are interested in it and likely to appear at any moment.

If the vendor absolutely refuses to see reason, you may well have to come back much later to make your point and get the object at your price, but this strategy requires great nerve and has been known to fail.

Outdoor Markets

Although some of the above techniques can be used at outdoor markets, in the main they are generally relaxed affairs where a much more jocular type of bartering takes place and where it is possible to get remarkable bargains.

There are drawbacks, though. You need to be up at the crack of dawn to get the best bargains and, generally speaking, outdoor markets are held in fields, where the mud squelches underfoot in the winter and where the sun beats down mercilessly in the summer. This can all be counteracted, however, by acquiring an alarm clock, some thermal underwear, a pair of wellington boots and a sun hat. In addition to these essential pieces of equipment you might also consider investing in a money bag or belt to wear around your waist. This is not so much to deter pickpockets as to leave both hands free for the scrummage and for the carrying of purchases.

Garage Sales

Garage sales are usually very informal family affairs where it is sometimes possible to get fabulous bargains, but where occasionally you run up against families with delusions of grandeur, who will ask the earth for a cracked fish tank. In the main, though, they are worth arriving early for, but make sure you take plenty of plastic bags and small change . . . they don't usually have either.

'For Sale' Columns in Newspapers

As you will see later in the book, it is absolutely essential to be one of the first to get your local newspaper if you intend to buy from it. This can mean bribing the newspaper boy to start his round at your house or, if he doesn't get the papers early enough, it might mean going to the newspaper offices and picking one up personally.

Once you have found an item that interests you, make an appointment to view it, but never go alone. It is important to take someone with you, not only because you are going to a strange house and don't want to be whisked off and never seen again, but also because you will need a second opinion and someone to give you moral support if you don't like what you see and find it difficult to leave.

Choose this companion with great care; it is no good taking anyone who is likely to gush and enthuse the minute the item is produced for you to look at. You really need someone rather reserved who has your best interests at heart, and who will not be averse to pointing out any possible faults or drawbacks in the piece, especially if they pertain to price.

Junk Shops

Junk shops are usually called 'antique shops' these days, which often means that they do up their own junk and sell it as antiques. This practice makes them extremely reluctant to sell you any honest-to-goodness junk, although occasionally you will come across an 'antique dealer' with a sense of fair play who will allow you to rummage through his back room.

You will also find lots of 'designer junk' in such shops which is mainly pine, highly waxed or smothered in antiquing fluid. Not only is such junk very expensive to buy, but you will also discover that antiquing fluid is an absolute bind to clean off!

Charity Shops

Charity shops used to be a wonderful source of junk until some of them grew into such big and complex organizations that they are now barely distinguishable from ordinary shops. I never bother with these when I am looking for junk, but I do regularly visit some of the smaller ones that specialize in furniture and where you can still pick up a bargain.

Remember, though, that for some obscure reason it is considered to be acting in extremely bad taste if you try to get the price reduced in a charity shop!

Other Outlets

Jumble/Rummage Sales You are bound to come back bruised from professionally flailing elbows, but it could be worth the trip.

Auction Sales Go to the viewing day and tick in your catalogue the pieces you find interesting. Beside them write down your absolute limit price-wise.

Then on the day, sit on your hands!

Cards in Newsagent's Windows See "For Sale" Columns in Newspapers' opposite, and make sure that the card is genuine and not in code for something unmentionable.

I hope that these few tips on junk collecting will come in useful and that you will find the acquisition and renovation of junk as satisfying as I do. I guarantee that you will never feel the same again about buying something new. Meekly handing over the right money for something which is going to be delivered wrapped and ready to use always seems a bit tame after the thrill of the chase and the smell of the oil paint!

Equipment & Materials

This might look like an incredible mixture of tools and materials, but you probably own most of them already. If you do need to buy any, however, remember *that you can pick up tools, paints, fabrics and trimmings at the same sort of venues as you can pick up junk, and just as cheaply!*

I have used a tremendous variety of equipment and materials in this book, from liming wax to dressmaker's pins. Looking through the lists at the beginning of each project, you could be forgiven for thinking that, although the junk may be cheap, doing it up could involve a second mortgage! This need not be so, however, if you extend your bargain hunting to tins of paint, brushes, rolls of fabric, etc. All of these things turn up, brand new, in the self same outlets I have described in the introduction.

There is an air of opportunism to this type of shopping I admit, but over the months you will find that with a little forward planning and a judicious approach to stock-piling you will usually be able to go to your shed or work-room and find exactly what you need.

Preparatory Materials

PAINT & VARNISH STRIPPERS

Both are very caustic and best put on with an old house-painting brush and wearing rubber gloves. Follow the instructions on the bottle to the letter and don't be tempted to start the scraping off too soon. Use a purpose-made, multi-edged scraper to remove the paint and varnish or, when you get desperate, anything else that looks as if it might do the job!

SANDPAPER & WIRE WOOL

Sandpaper and wire wool are produced in all grades from very fine to coarse and are used in a variety of ways from stripping wood to lightly sanding a final coat of varnish.

Some abrasive papers may be used wet or dry and the fine ones are particularly good for getting a smooth surface between layers while preparing a base coat. These papers do produce quite a slurry however and, as this can prevent you from seeing exactly how much surface has been removed, I never use them on a decorated surface and am very careful on a plain one.

Wire wool is also a very useful abrasive and may be used on either wood or metal. It is particularly useful when used in conjunction with a stripper for removing old varnish and paint from turned legs and awkward corners. I recommend using fine wire wool, which is labelled as either 000 or 0000 gauge.

TACK RAG

Tack rags are lint-free, extremely tacky rags that are essential for wiping over a recently sanded surface, as they pick up all the dust and grit left behind by rubbing down with sandpaper. They are very easy to get hold of now in builders' suppliers and will make all the difference to the finish of your work. When you are not using it, keep your tack rag in a jam jar with a screw-top lid and always shake it out well before using it again.

When using emulsion paint, use a lint-free rag wrung out in warm water as a tack rag.

WOOD FILLER

Most brands of wood filler come in a variety of wood tints, so that if the finish you are using is not going to cover the wood completely any repair will be less obvious. Generally, though, any quick-drying, neutral-coloured wood filler will suit most problems.

Fine cracks, small holes and rough wood grain are usually better dealt with using fine surface polyfiller.

WOOD GLUE

I find that Evo-Stick Wood Adhesive is the solution to most wood sticking problems and many others as well. For example, you could use it to stick on the shells in the bathroom mirror project (see page 00).

PVA GLUE

This is a thoroughly well-behaved glue, which I sometimes think can do absolutely anything. Apart from the face that it glues things together very firmly and dries quickly and transparently, it may also be used slightly diluted as a stiffener for fabrics, as a varnish or sealer or even as a medium for binding powder paints. It is also non-toxic, very cheap and available just about everywhere – an essential for your shopping list!

SANDING SEALER

Sanding sealer is used to seal wood before various paint finishes and for a variety of reasons. I have used it in this book to stop varnish discolouring a pale colourwash (see page 43) and to prevent liming wax penetrating areas other than the grain on the oak chest (see page 59).

Brushes

Wherever possible you should always buy the best you can afford, or maybe I should say the best that are on offer. Always buy recognizable brands and, if you are buying them under slightly dubious circumstances, give them a good tug to make sure that all the hairs are fixed firmly into the ferrule.

HOUSE-PAINTING BRUSHES

I have used 2.5cm (1in) and 4cm (1½in) house-painting brushes for most of the base painting in this book, whether I have been using oil-based or emulsion paints. Where I have used a colourwash, though, and needed to flood areas with much thinner paint I have found a 5cm (2in) brush more useful.

VARNISHING BRUSH

Choose a fat, silky brush for varnishing so that you can paint on varnish and leave the minimum of brush strokes. Then, once you have chosen your brush, remain ever faithful to it and never use it for anything else other than varnishing.

ARTIST'S BRUSHES

Artist's brushes are made from a variety of materials and one of the most desirable and expensive is sable. A fine sable brush is wonderful for veining marble or painting freehand designs on furniture in either oils or designer colours, but never subject the poor thing to acrylics or to the cellulose thinners used with enamel paints because these will ruin it completely.

The manufacturers of artist's brushes make several reasonable synthetic alternatives to sable brushes, some of which are specifically recommended for acrylic paints, and all of which work well with other paints. They are not so flexible as sables, though, and are quick to lose their points.

ARTIST'S LINING BRUSHES

Artist's lining brushes, sometimes called 'stripers' or even 'calligraphy brushes', are used to produce long, even lines on pieces of furniture. They are long and thin in shape so that they can hold a quantity of paint. As these brushes can take a bit of getting used to, it is advisable to have a preliminary practice on a piece of paper before painting on furniture.

Artist's lining brushes are available from specialist paint stores and art shops.

STENCIL BRUSHES

Stencil brushes are short and stubby and are usually made from some kind of bristle or hog's hair. They come in more sizes than you would expect and are available in most DIY outlets, although you will get more of a selection in one of the many specialist stencilling shops that are beginning to appear.

SOFTENERS

I use a badger softener to blur the veining and soften the brush strokes on marbling and similar finishes, but I must admit it is an old friend and it cost a fortune when I bought it many years ago.

Badger softeners are even more expensive now, but you can get them in smaller sizes or you could content yourself with a bristle softener or even a brush known as a duster. If you are on a real economy drive, you could try using an old badger shaving brush or a large, soft cosmetic brush.

WIRE BRUSH

This is used for loosening really bad rust or for opening up the grain on oak or similar woods, prior to liming. Wire brushes are very inexpensive and available in most hardware or DIY shops.

NATURAL SPONGE

A natural sponge is preferable for sponging as it will give your work the desired random effect. Synthetic sponges have holes which are far too regular and clean-cut. Natural sponges are much more expensive, of course, particularly if you buy them at a chemist. Builders' merchants that sell specialist materials are a much cheaper source . . . or you could take your holidays in Greece.

Paints, Primers & Undercoats

This group of materials turns up in abundance at open-air markets and they are worth checking over to see if they are still in good condition. I never buy anything but the well-known brands and always open the tin to see how much paint is in there and what state it is in.

PRIMERS

Use a wood primer on new or stripped wood to seal it and to prevent subsequent coats of paint from sinking into the grain. Give metal which has been stripped or rubbed back one or two coats of red oxide.

UNDERCOATS

Many of the modern oil-based paints no longer need an undercoat, but if you do decide to use one, it goes over the primer and under the first layer of base coat. It is definitely not necessary if you are working on a sound surface which already has an old layer of paint or varnish, unless it is a particularly intrusive colour – in which case the undercoat will help to mask it.

EMULSION PAINTS

Emulsion paints are water based and relatively quick drying. In this book I have used them thinned down to colourwash furniture, and thickened up to verdigris metal. They could also be used as an alternative base for découpage (see page 68), or tinted and rubbed back on the kitchen table and chair (see page 26).

Emulsion paint is extraordinarily versatile, but if you intend to use it as a base for freehand decorative painting, it is a good idea to paint a coat of clear varnish over the emulsion before you start, as it is very porous and mistakes are difficult to remove. To tint emulsion, use water-based paints such as designer colours.

OIL-BASED HOUSEHOLD PAINTS

Oil-based paints come in flat, eggshell and gloss finishes. Gloss paint is not used very often for decorative finishes, particularly if you are hoping to make the thing look old and worn. Flat oil-based paint is only available in a very limited colour range. Therefore eggshell and mid-sheen finishes are the ones most often used, both as base coats and to make glazes for decorative finishes.

Oil-based paints give a much tougher finish than emulsion paints and are particularly useful in light-coloured glazes where a scumble glaze and the addition of varnish would be too yellowing. The only drawback to oil-based paints is that they take a long time to dry and need 24 hours between coats.

To tint oil-based paints, use artist's oil paints or universal stainers which are stronger and cheaper, but not quite so subtle.

ARTIST'S OIL COLOURS

Artist's oil paints may be mixed with any oil-based paint or glaze to tint it, but they are slow drying and they will slightly delay the drying time of anything they are mixed with.

However, they are the most subtle and magical of paints and in theory can be used for almost any decorative finish from barge painting to stencilling, although it is usually the quicker drying media which are used in practice.

If you are good at painting, nothing is better than oils for painting small, old-fashioned rural scenes with scrolled borders on otherwise boring pieces of furniture. It quite transforms an old varnished piece, even if you do nothing else to it.

ARTIST'S ACRYLIC PAINTS

Artist's acrylic paints come in tubes and may be mixed to create any colour you desire, but if you are repeating your design, or need to cover a fairly large area with acrylics, it is probably better to buy the ready-mixed acrylic craft paints which come in pots. Using these will save you the problem of having to mix exactly the right colour every time.

Acrylic paints dry very quickly and are particularly suited to stencilling, although you will need to wash your stencil often to avoid paint building up around the edges. You will also need to make sure that your brushes never dry out with acrylic paint on them.

Acrylics may be applied over either emulsion or oil-based paints.

DESIGNER COLOURS (GOUACHE)

Designer colours are water based and are meant to be used in an opaque fashion, although you may water them down considerably.

Designer colours can be used for tinting emulsion paints or for painting designs onto emulsion paint, especially on a colourwash. A perfect example of painting onto a colourwashed background can be seen in the dining room table project (see page 44).

It is possible to use designer colours on an oil-based paint, but you will probably need to rub the surface down lightly to give it a 'key' and add a little washing-up liquid to the paint to make it adhere. Designer colours are very easy to move when they are on an oil-based paint and for that reason it is a good idea to apply one coat of spray varnish to fix them before laying on subsequent coats of varnish with a brush.

SPRAY PAINTS

I have used some specialized spray paint on the garden furniture project (see page 88) because it is so wonderful at getting around all the scrolls and curls in wrought iron. Painting wrought iron takes an absolute eternity to do with a paintbrush and you usually end up missing something out. I have also used spray paint on wickerwork because it is less likely to clog up the holes in the weave (see page 80).

There is no reason why you should not use spray paint on most of the furniture and objects in this book, except that it is more difficult to control than a brush and it is possible to spray the surrounding surfaces without really meaning to.

Whenever you use spray paint it is always better to apply several thin coats of paint and to let each one dry before applying the next. If you try to apply too much at one time it might look alright to begin with, but will soon start to drip.

Spray paint may be used very successfully with stencils and you can get some really lovely effects by gradating the colours on the edges of flowers and leaves.

ENAMEL PAINTS

I find that enamel paints are the best thing for barge painting, particularly if you are working on metal. They go on very smoothly and dry fairly quickly, although they do need to be stirred thoroughly before use.

They have their own cellulose thinners to thin them and to act as a solvent, but you will find that these thinners are particularly hard on brushes and that white spirit makes a reasonable and gentler alternative.

POWDER PAINTS

Powder paints are finely ground pigment and I have used them to make a colourwash for the kitchen table and chair project (see page 26).

Although they are wonderful for tinting emulsions, glazes and even varnishes, powder paints are not actually water soluble and ideally should be ground into a paste with a little water before being made into a colourwash or added to emulsion. Provided you keep stirring the mix while you work, however, it is possible to miss out the pestle and mortar stage.

BRONZING POWDERS

I have used gold bronzing powder on several projects throughout this book and generally used acrylic varnish as a mixing medium so that I can paint it on. An alternative would be to shake it onto semi-dry gold size. Either way, it really needs a further coat of varnish to prevent it from going dull.

UNIVERSAL STAINERS

Although universal stainers do not have the range of subtle colours that oil paints and designer colours have, they will mix with virtually everything . . . water-based and oil-based alike. They also have the distinct advantage of being very cheap.

They come in liquid form and are extremely strong, so either dilute them or add them to any mixture with great care. I used them to tint the polyurethane varnish for the deck chair (see page 92).

Varnishes & Glazes

POLYURETHANE VARNISH

Polyurethane varnish is like oil-based paint in that it comes in matt, satin and gloss finishes. It is a very handy and versatile varnish and I have used it in most of the projects, either from a tin or in spray form for finishes which were best left undisturbed by brushes.

It dries to a very hard-wearing surface, but tends to give a yellowish cast to whatever it is covering.

TRANSPARENT OIL GLAZE

The most beautiful effects can be obtained by mixing oil-based paints of one kind or another with a transparent oil glaze. Although ragging, sponging and marbling (see page 75) can be attempted with other paints, nothing gives quite the same subtlety and softness as an oil glaze.

Nothing is perfect, however, and it does have a tendency to yellow in sunlight. It is also not a very robust finish and will usually need a coat of varnish which may also tend to yellow the finish slightly.

PAINT GLAZE

Because transparent oil glazes do have a tendency to yellow and inevitably need at least one coat of varnish to protect them, it is sometimes desirable to make a glaze which doesn't have either of these problems.

Ordinary eggshell paint mixed in equal quantities with white spirit and tinted with artist's oil colours makes quite an acceptable alternative. However, as it does not contain so much oil, it will not stay workable for as long and will not have the same luminous transparency as an oil glaze.

CRACKLE VARNISH

This will transform even the most boring piece of painted furniture into something which looks interestingly ancient. It is easy to obtain from most art shops and comes in a pack containing one bottle of slow-drying varnish, which is usually tinted, and one bottle of fast-drying varnish which is the one that cracks (see page 24).

ACRYLIC VARNISH

Acrylic varnish is one of the clearest varnishes available on the market and generally comes in a gloss or eggshell finish. It is water based and if you are using it on a piece of furniture which is going to receive a lot of wear and tear, such as a table or chair, it will generally need at least one protective coat, preferably two, of oil-based polyurethane varnish on top.

Wax

BEESWAX FURNITURE POLISH

A final coat or two of clear wax polish gives a lovely deep sheen to most pieces, particularly if you have used a matt or satin finish varnish.

I wax polish my work as often as possible and the surface just goes on getting better and better. Polishing with a good-quality tinted wax will also give your work quite a passable antiqued finish.

LIMING WAX

Liming wax is available in tins and is simply wax with the addition of a white pigment. By rubbing it into the grain of woods such as oak or ash you can quickly create a very soft and subtle finish.

White Spirit & Methylated Spirits

White spirit is a substitute for turpentine and may be used to dilute any oil-based paint or glaze. It may also be used as a solvent for removing oil paint and varnish from clothes and brushes, etc, or for cleaning old pieces of furniture with a pad of fine wire wool.

Methylated spirits may also be used with a pad of wire wool for rubbing down and cleaning pieces of furniture; this combination is especially useful when you are trying to remove sticky layers of french polish. Methylated spirits is also used in this book in the recipe for verdigris (see page 85).

Knives

I use a flexible-ended palette knife for a great many things, from mixing up artist's oil colours on a palette to applying wood filler. Strictly speaking, the very flexible, finely shaped knives are painting knives and you will find them for sale in most art shops. Buy one . . . they are quite indispensable.

You will need a sharp craft knife or scalpel for cutting out your stencils and once again it really does pay to get the best, which is a scalpel with interchangeable blades. You will find these in most art and craft shops but, sad to relate, I have never seen them in a junk market.

Scissors

You will need a good pair of dressmaker's scissors to attempt the soft furnishing projects in this book. You will also need a good pair of curved nail scissors if you intend to try découpage (see page 68), although you may decide to use a scalpel and cutting mat for that project.

Cutting Mat

When you are cutting stencils you will need a cutting board of some kind and, although you may be able to make do with an old chopping board or some such thing, there is nothing quite as wonderful as one of the Japanese self-healing cutting boards to work on. They come in several sizes and are readily available in art and craft shops but, dare I say it, they are quite expensive!

Plastic Film for Stencilling

This can prove fairly elusive if you do not live near a specialist stencilling shop, although most art and craft shops will order it for you if they don't actually keep it in stock. I have also found it for sale in dressmaking shops and haberdashery departments where it is known as plastic film for making patchwork templates.

It comes in various thicknesses and shapes and, if you really get carried away, you can buy it in rolls, although they are fairly hard to find.

Masking Tape, Drawing Paper & Tracing Paper

These are all self-explanatory and available in art and craft shops.

Buy good-quality tracing paper and low-tack masking tape, particularly if you are going to use it over an oil glaze. If you cannot get low-tack, try sticking strips of ordinary masking tape to your clothing before you use it and this should take off some of the stickiness.

Soft Furnishing Materials

Fabrics, piping cord, Velcro, etc are all available in any good soft furnishings shop or store and don't really need any further explanation.

I must add, though, that I have frequently seen all these items on specialist stalls in markets for a fraction of their shop prices. I have also bought some beautiful designer fabrics at garage sales.

Upholstery Materials & Tools

Upholstery tools are either available or can be ordered from most good tool shops. You will also find that upholsterers are usually only too willing to order you tools or sell you any of the specialist stuffing, tacks and braids, etc.

My local upholsterers are even friendlier and throw in free advice as well!

Techniques

Always make sure that you have all the materials to hand when you start a project, whether it involves painting or sewing. There is nothing worse than hunting for a rag with paint-covered hands or trying to hold a piece of loose cover in place while you look for the pins.

It is a fact of life that basic techniques such as rubbing down surfaces, stripping off old paint and wood filling take hours and hours to do properly while the really enjoyable jobs like sponging and freehand painting take no time at all. Unfortunately we can't really have one without the other and you have to learn to love the preparation as much as the decoration.

My defence against the less pleasant jobs is listening to the radio. I have found that if you tune in to the right station you can practically acquire a second education while you are working your way through the boring jobs. I've been listening to the radio for so long now that my legal advice is second to none and I'm the local authority on women's problems!

Stripping & Cleaning

If the piece you wish to decorate has a reasonably unbroken and well-applied layer of old paint or varnish on it there is no need to strip it unless the finish you are attempting calls for bare wood.

You may simply clean it down with white spirit and wire wool and then go over it with a clean cloth which has been wrung out in hot, soapy water. If it is a wooden object, don't drench it in water or it will raise the grain and require twice as much rubbing down.

If the surface is chipped and uneven, however, it will be necessary to strip everything off and start again.

If it is only a small piece that you are doing up, it is probably just as easy and economical to strip it yourself, but if you work out how many tins of stripper you will need for a large piece and then add on the wear and tear on the family (dogs, cats and toddlers appear as if by magic when you produce a tin of stripper) you may think it just as easy to take it to a professional.

Assuming that you do decide to pay a visit to a professional stripper, be sure that you find one who uses the 'cold chemical' non-caustic method of stripping. This will ensure that you will not only get your piece back with the minimum of rubbing down left to do, but you will also be able to take wicker pieces to him, provided that they are not too caked in paint.

If you decide to strip the piece yourself, clear the decks for action and put on a protective apron and a stout pair of rubber gloves.

There are several types of stripper available which are suitable for both metal and wood although you need to make sure that you have the correct one for either paint or varnish. You also need to make sure that you are actually dealing with varnish. It is sometimes difficult to know whether an item has been french polished or varnished until you try removing the finish with some methylated spirits on a wad of fine wire wool. If it is french polish it will come off in a sticky mess, but if it has been varnished you will only remove the surface dirt and nothing else.

Apply the stripper with an old paintbrush and follow the instructions on the tin to the letter. It will almost certainly tell you to wait longer than you think you should and then to add another coat of stripper and wait some more. The job will definitely be a lot easier if you follow this advice even though it is almost impossible not to have a surreptitious scrape in the meantime.

Gluing & Filling

Stripping off the old paint usually shows up any holes or loose pieces which may have been lurking and now is the time to fill them or glue them back. If you are planning to put a paint finish on your piece later, some quick-drying neutral-coloured wood filler will deal with most of the holes, but very small holes and coarse wood grain are often more easily filled with fine surface polyfiller.

If you are leaving the wood partly showing for any reason, for example liming or even colourwashing, it is better to fill the holes with a tinted wood filler.

Apply the filler with the flexible blade of a palette knife and leave it just a little proud of the surface so that you can rub it down level when it is dry.

Most gluing problems can be cured with the application of a good-quality wood adhesive and some form of clamp, weight or string to keep the repair in place while the glue is drying.

Rubbing Down

Whether you manage to retain the old surface or whether you have had to strip your piece, it will need rubbing down before you can go any further. It is very important that you spend some time and effort getting the best possible surface at this point because it is the basis upon which all your other efforts will rest.

When working with wood always try to use a sanding block. Wrap a piece of sandpaper around this and rub the item down with long firm strokes, using the whole of your arm and shoulder and going with the grain.

Alternatively you might like to use a wad of fine wire wool, although I usually reserve this for awkward corners and use ribbons of it for turned legs and edges. I also find the fine abrasive cloths which are available now very flexible and therefore useful for anything that has a rounded edge.

If you are decorating a metal piece some abrasive cloths are made specifically for metal and are particularly useful, although very fine wire wool also gives metal a wonderful finish.

When you have finished rubbing down, whether it is wood or metal, go over the piece with your tack rag to make sure that there is no debris left over from the rubbing down process.

Priming & Painting

If you are dealing with a wooden item that has been stripped, it will have to be primed before you can proceed with painting it. If it is going to be colourwashed or limed it will first need to be treated with sanding sealer (see page 59).

Metal objects which have been stripped will need to be primed with red oxide unless they are going to receive a finish such as verdigris (see page 85).

When the objects have been primed and allowed to dry they will need to be rubbed down lightly and dusted with a tack rag before being painted.

Paint Finishes

SPONGING

I used sponging in two of the projects in this book – the nest of tables in the living room (see page 60) and the wicker items in the bathroom (see page 80). Although the technique sounds the same in both cases, in fact the materials and the processes were quite different.

The tables were given an eggshell base coat consisting of several layers of paint and allowed to dry. They were

◄ Rubbing down
To rub down wooden furniture, wrap a piece of sandpaper around a cork block and use this to rub down the furniture with long, firm strokes, always going with the grain.

◄ Priming metal
Before painting a metallic surface, prime it with two coats of red oxide to ensure that the metal remains free of rust, and then allow to dry.

▲Painting wood
Paint in the direction of the grain wherever possible, checking there are no drips. Allow the base coat to dry before applying a second coat.

The beauty of the 'sponging on' technique is that a second or even a third colour may be added, either while the first colour is still wet or for a slightly more defined texture, when it has dried.

Both the eggshell paint glaze and the transparent oil glaze may be used to sponge on or off.

BAGGING

Bagging is a variation of sponging using a scrunched-up plastic bag instead of a sponge (see the plant stand on page 62). You may use either the eggshell glaze or the transparent oil glaze to get this effect. Try experimenting with different types and thicknesses of paper or plastic bag.

STIPPLING

See the plant stand (page 62). I used a short-bristled emulsion brush to stipple into an eggshell glaze for this project, but you could just as easily use a transparent oil glaze and a purpose-made stippling brush. Don't worry about buying a stippling brush unless you are going to make a career out of stippling, though, because they are horrendously expensive.

MARBLING

See the dressing table (page 75). The marble used in this project is really a fantasy marble and would never appear in real life. If you find it difficult to invent a marble or would like something which looked more realistic, try copying an actual piece of marble, but keep it simple to start with. Highly coloured marble with elaborate veining is really quite a skilled job and you will need a little more expert help before attempting it.

FAUX TORTOISESHELL

See the lamp base and shade (page 64). Once again this is a fantasy or false tortoiseshell effect, but you could try copying the real thing, if you have something which is made from it. You will find that the colours vary enormously and you may have to alter the base coat to ochre, red or even green.

then painted section by section with a tinted paint glaze, that is an equal amount of white spirit and eggshell paint, tinted with artist's oil paints.

The pattern was made by 'sponging off' or by pouncing a clean natural sponge over the glaze in a random fashion until the tables were completely covered in the textured pattern of the sponge. Because the sponge was taking glaze off each time it was pounced onto the tables, it was necessary to clean it regularly on a piece of clean cloth.

If you are covering larger areas, however, it may be desirable to rinse the sponge out in white spirit followed by warm, soapy water now and then, but make sure that you dry it thoroughly before re-using it.

The wicker linen basket and wastepaper basket in the bathroom were first spray-painted and then the sponge was used to 'sponge on' a diluted mixture of acrylic paint. In this case the paint was taken up on the sponge and any surplus was dabbed onto a spare piece of paper before the sponge was pounced randomly over the wicker. The sponge should be twisted and turned as you work so that it does not make a uniform pattern.

PORPHYRY

See the set of three picture frames (page 49). Porphyry is really a version of spattering. In this project I have suggested you use a stencil brush to get the right effect, but you could just as easily use a toothbrush or hold a stick of wood parallel to your work and bang the handle of a paint-laden paintbrush against it.

Try different methods and different colours and you will be surprised at the effects you can achieve, but watch out for the drips!

COLOURWASH

See the emulsion paint colourwash on the sideboard (page 42) and the powder paint colourwash on the kitchen table and chair (page 26). This is one of the easiest finishes and one of the most popular, although you will always get the occasional visitor who will say, 'When are you going to put another coat on it?'

VERDIGRIS

See the bathroom mirror and door handles (page 85). I love this finish and it really is very simple to do once you have all your pastes made up. I must warn you, though, that methylated spirits can make you feel quite giddy, so keep a window open if you are working indoors.

LIMING

See the oak chest (page 59). I waxed this chest when it was finished because liming wax cannot be varnished. If you wanted a similar finish which could be varnished or even stencilled over, the simplest alternative would be a colourwash.

Decorative Finishes

BARGE PAINTING

See the old iron pot (page 34) and brush stroke illustrations (pages 36–7). Once you have mastered the basic brush strokes of any folk art, the world is your oyster and

◄**Stippling**
Holding a stiff decorator's brush upright, pounce it all over a surface of wet glaze to create the typical stippled pattern of tiny dots.

◄**Verdigris**
After applying verdigris pastes and sieved whiting, rub back some of the piece to its base coat with a cloth and leave to dry.

you can, and do, go around decorating anything that stands still long enough. It is only practice that will bring about that happy state of events, however, and I would suggest that you buy a few off-cuts of hardboard and prime and paint them, so that you can practise your brush strokes for a while before starting your project.

DÉCOUPAGE

See the headboard (page 68). Although cutting out pictures and gluing them on sounds easier than actually painting them, there is still quite a craft to découpage and you must make sure that you prepare the smoothest of base coats to glue them on to and several equally smooth layers of varnish to cover them with.

STENCILLING

See the bedroom chair for designing, cutting and applying a stencil (page 70). If designing and making your own stencil really does not appeal to you there are so many beautiful ready-made designs available that you are bound to find one to suit your purpose.

CRACKLE VARNISH

Crackle varnish gives a very ancient and crazed look to even the freshest of decorative finishes and looks its best over handpainted or découpaged designs.

You can buy the two bottles of varnish which are necessary to make a crackle varnish effect in most art and craft shops, but make sure that you pick up both varnishes, because they are quite often packaged separately. You will need one bottle labelled 'ageing' or 'antiquing varnish' and one labelled 'crackleur' or 'cracking varnish'.

The crackle varnish must always be applied over a nonporous surface, so make sure that you have covered your work with at least one coat of oil-based polyurethane varnish and allowed it to dry thoroughly.

To get the crackled effect first paint on the antiquing varnish, then apply the cracking varnish when the first is almost dry. This is the point when most people come unstuck, because the instructions can be very difficult to interpret; and a great deal also depends on the prevailing atmosphere. My advice is to wait until you can just touch the first coat of varnish without leaving a fingerprint. You will need to keep testing this in a spot that doesn't show because if you leave it too long and the varnish dries it will not crackle.

The second coat of varnish is water based and dries very quickly. The cracking occurs because the first layer continues to dry and move about long after the second has dried. If there are no signs of cracking after an hour or so you may help things on their way by gently applying a little heat from a hair dryer, but don't hold the dryer too close and stop as soon as the cracks appear.

When both layers are completely dry, mix a little Raw Umber artist's oil paint with a very small amount of Jet Black oil paint and add enough white spirit to make a milky consistency. Apply this mix to the work and leave it until it begins to lose its shine, but do not let it dry.

Take a clean, *dry* brush and work the mixture well into the cracks, wiping the excess off the brush all the time with a clean rag. Chop up some old nylon stockings or tights and make these up into little pads. Go over the antiquing with these, using a circular motion and changing them frequently as they get dirty.

Leave plenty of paint in the cracks, but arrange the rest of the antiquing fluid so that it is denser in places where you would normally expect dirt to have gathered over the ages. Conversely, rub it well back where the piece might have been touched a lot. When the antiquing is quite dry, apply one more coat of matt polyurethane varnish.

Soft Furnishing Techniques

See the kitchen chair (page 26), dining room chairs (page 46), garden chairs (page 89) and the ottoman (page 73) for details on making and re-upholstering seat cushions. The dressing table project (page 75) gives details on making curtains, while the deck chair (page 92) explains how to replace old chair fabric. For making loose covers, see the account in the three-piece suite project (page 54).

The Kitchen

There is never any shortage of small pine pieces to buy at second-hand markets and they make excellent objects on which to practise folk art. This type of

painting is so attractive that even your first efforts will probably look good enough to keep.

My kitchen attracts junk like a magnet. I am forever picking up bits that I simply cannot resist and, although I know that I don't really *need* them, I manage to convince myself that they are unique bargains which will never come my way again. So, sensibly, I strike while the iron is hot!

Once home, these 'finds' are optimistically carted around the house until, failing to fit in anywhere else, they are temporarily stored in the kitchen. There they sit, looking totally out of place, waiting for inspiration or a needy friend to strike.

Although most of the junk collected for this kitchen had at least the virtue of *looking* culinary, the pieces still needed some kind of treatment to unify them. I therefore

▲ The kitchen table
The kitchen table was an old friend that had seen many incarnations.

▼ The church chair
Old church chairs make an interesting alternative to plain kitchen chairs.

chose a rustic theme using colourwashes and plenty of naive decoration for the wooden pieces. The metal pot and the key holder I treated to a splash of colour, smothering them with the traditional British folk art usually associated with barge painting.

Highly decorative pieces like these will instantly give your kitchen a cosy cottagey feel, particularly if you complement them with plain, whitewashed walls and some pretty curtains.

Kitchen Table & Chair

I always think of this old kitchen table when I hear the expression 'like part of the furniture' – meaning that something or somebody seems to have been around for ever. This little pine table has been with me in various guises since my long-departed student days when it was bought as part of a cheap job lot to furnish a flat.

It was originally covered in some particularly foul linoleum and I thought I was doing it a great favour when I stripped that off and re-covered it with some equally noxious formica, which in turn gave way to gleaming white paint, stripped pine, and finally a trendy, cream colourwash.

I'd like to think that this gorgeous, rustic colourwash and handpainting was its last incarnation, but somehow I doubt it.

The little church chair is a fairly recent acquisition which I bought for a reasonable price in a borderline junk/antique shop. This one is particularly pretty but I have seen masses of slightly plainer ones going, quite literally, for next to nothing.

MATERIALS
Fine grade sandpaper
Tack rag
White emulsion paint
2 x 4cm (1½in) house-painting brushes
Fine wire wool
Methylated spirits
Cloths
Red Oxide powder paint
Raw Umber powder paint
Polyurethane spray varnish
Your chosen design
Tracing paper
Pencil
Acrylic paints
Artist's paintbrush
Clear, matt polyurethane varnish

As the kitchen table had already been colourwashed quite recently, it really only needed a quick rub down with some fine sandpaper and a dust with the tack rag and it was ready for painting.

I then gave it two coats of white emulsion paint, which I rubbed down and tacked after the last layer was completely dry. I dealt with the little church chair in the same way although, because it had the dust and dirt of ages on it, I first cleaned it thoroughly with fine wire wool and methylated spirits, followed by a wipe over with a cloth wrung out in hot, soapy water, before I painted it.

MAKING THE COLOURWASH
I mixed approximately three teaspoonfuls of the Red Oxide powder paint with a very small amount of the Raw Umber and added enough water to make a creamy mix. (If you own a pestle and mortar, you could grind the pigment into the water at this stage to make it more soluble.)

I then continued to add approximately 155ml (5fl oz) of water because I wanted quite a strong pink, but you could add a little more water to make a paler wash.

APPLYING THE WASH
Tipping the table upside down, and dealing with the legs first, I painted the wash onto the table with one of the house-painting brushes.

I think it is always safest to start with the legs so that the all-important top of the table is the last thing you paint

▶ **Tracing the design**
I photocopied a page from a book on old decorations in several different sizes, so that I could use the same design on both the kitchen chair and table. When I had decided exactly where I wanted to place them, I traced off the appropriate sizes so that I could then copy them back onto the furniture.

and therefore (a) doesn't get disturbed again and (b) has the benefit of you having had a practice on the not-so-obvious table legs!

Having completed the legs, I allowed a few minutes for the wash to begin to dry before going over it again with a clean, dry brush so that I could work the wash into the grain and take off any surplus. It is important not to be too heavy-handed with this process and also to make sure that you keep cleaning your brush on a dry rag while you are working. Finally I gently buffed over the legs with a clean, dry cloth, before up-ending the table and treating the top in the same way.

A colourwash of this kind is extremely fragile and can easily be rubbed off or 'dripped' upon at this stage so it is very important to get it under a protective layer of spray varnish as soon as possible.

It is not advisable to use varnish from a tin as this colourwash is *so* vulnerable that putting varnish on with a brush is likely to move the wash and make it streaky. I therefore gave the table several *light* coats of spray varnish.

ADDING DECORATION

I had already chosen a simple black and white design from a book of classical patterns, which I thought would adapt to make both a border for the table and a decorative motif for the chair. To use the same design on both the small chair back and the relatively large table area I had the design photocopied in various sizes so that it would fit wherever I wanted to put it. I then traced the strips of design and transferred them onto the furniture (see page 61) before colouring them in with acrylic paints.

The design I had chosen was extremely simple and only required three acrylic colours to paint it, but as it is this simplicity that gives rustic furniture its air of naive elegance, try not to choose a pattern that is too complicated in design or sophisticated in colour.

As I had already protected the colourwash with spray varnish, I was now at liberty to use a brush and paint the table and chair with clear, matt polyurethane varnish to protect the design, once the acrylic paint had dried.

▶ **Arranging the design**
It is helpful to cut out the various design elements and move them around until you find the perfect arrangement.

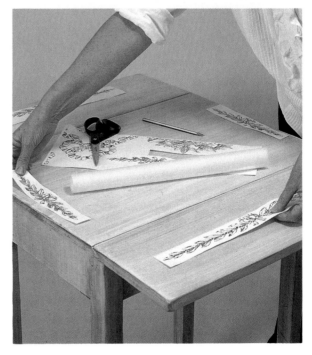

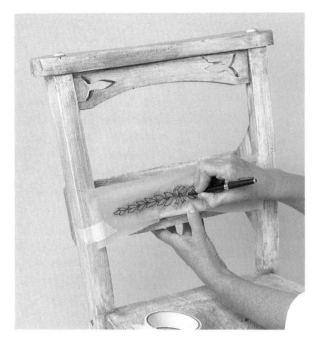

Cushion

I think that most of us have become painfully aware at some time in our lives of how unforgivingly hard these little church chairs can be and how desperately they need a cushion! The idea for this one came from a very old American film.

MATERIALS
Old newspaper
Masking tape
Tracing paper
Pencil
Scissors
1m (40in) suitable material
1m (40in) contrasting material
Approximately 25cm (10in) thick polyester wadding
Cotton
Needle
Pins
Approximately 3m (10ft) No.3 piping cord
Tape measure
25cm (10in) Velcro fastener

MAKING THE PATTERN
Even on something as simple as a chair seat I like to make a newspaper pattern, especially if it is a design which I have not attempted before. I made this pattern by taping a large sheet of newspaper to the seat of the chair and then tracing carefully around the edge with the side of a pencil. I drew a curved shape around the back struts and then cut out the pattern. To make sure that the pattern was completely symmetrical, I folded it in two and trimmed off any discrepancies.

MAKING THE COVER
I used the pattern to cut out one thickness of the main fabric, one of the contrasting fabric and one of the polyester wadding. I sandwiched the wadding between the two pieces of fabric so that the right sides were facing out-

◀ **Transferring a design**
After I had scribbled on the back of the tracing with a soft pencil, I taped it in place and transferred the design to the back of the chair by going over it with the hard point of a ballpoint pen.

◀ **Painting the design**
As I had already varnished the chair to protect the delicate colourwash, I painted the design with acrylic paints. The design was kept very simple, in keeping with the chair.

wards and basted across the middle from top to bottom and from side to side to hold the pieces in place.

Using the contrasting fabric and the piping cord, I then prepared enough covered cord to go around the top of the chair seat twice (see page 91).

I also cut a further strip of contrasting fabric on the cross (approximately 25cm x 4cm/10in x 1½in). This I folded in half lengthwise and pressed once before folding both the raw edges into the middle and pressing again. I cut this strip of binding in half and used each piece to bind the curves cut for the back struts, by first basting and then machining them in place.

I then measured around the front three sides of the chair and, adding on 20cm (8in) for the fixing flaps, I cut a strip of the main material this length and 7.5cm (3in) deep. Laying this strip right side up and starting and finishing 10cm (4in) from either end, I pinned on a length of piping so that all the raw edges were together and then basted the pieces together.

I measured the fabric representing the space between the two struts at the back of the chair and, adding 2.5cm (1in) onto the length for hemming, I cut another 7.5cm (3in) deep strip and piped as before. Using the rest of the piping cord and the same method, I then sewed piping cord along the other sides of both strips.

MAKING THE FRILL

I then cut several more 7.5cm (3in) deep strips of material until, by joining them together, I had two long strips, each one approximately three times longer than the two piped strips. I hemmed each of these along one long side and two short sides. The remaining sides I gathered until they were as long as the piped sections of the first two strips.

With right sides and the raw edges together, I first basted and then machined the long frill to the piped section of the longest strip and then attached the short one to the shortest strip.

To attach these frilled sections to the seat cover, I pinned the unattached, piped side of the long frill around the front three sides of the seat cover and the shorter one in a similar manner to the fourth side, between the two curves cut for the back struts. I then basted and machined them in place.

Finally I hemmed the fixing tabs at either end of the long frill band and both sides of the back frill band before attaching the Velcro fastener. This was so the tabs would fit around behind the back struts of the chair.

FINISHING TOUCHES

Once the chair was painted and had its cushion in place, the little box at the back which had once held hymn books, began to cry out to be filled. As it was now a kitchen chair I did consider filling the box with cookery books or magazines, but that wasn't really glamorous enough for it. I finally decided upon dried lavender and rose-buds, which I packed in tightly and sprayed with preservative to stop the petals dropping off.

▲Pine objects
These items abound at junk markets and look best decorated with folk art or naive designs.

Pine Shelf, Spice Rack & Spoon Holder

When you are wandering around outdoor and flea markets, little pine objects such as these seem to be every-where and the funny thing is that, although you might well have thrown something similar away only weeks before, the compulsion to buy someone else's cast-offs is overwhelming.

It must have something to do with the lure of pine, which always looks attractive whatever you do with it, but particularly when you evoke its Scandinavian connec-tions. This is exactly what I did with these pine pieces which I decorated with a soft, dusty turquoise, a colour which almost inevitably turns up on old Swedish furni-ture.

I have taken the painted design from a very pretty, old plate which also forced itself upon me at a flea market and which has been beautifully decorated by hand, using brush strokes similar to the ones on pages 36–7.

MATERIALS
Wood filler
Palette knife
Medium and fine sandpaper
Tack rag
Designer colours (gouache):
Ultramarine, Lemon Yellow, Raw Umber
Jam jar
Old tablespoon
White emulsion paint
2 x 4cm (1½in) house-painting brushes
Paper & pencil
Clear, matt polyurethane varnish
Artist's paintbrush
Acrylic paints
Washing-up liquid
Fine wire wool
Cotton buds
Bleach
Lint-free rag

PINE SHELF
The pine shelf had obviously once been painted white and had survived a half-hearted attempt to strip it – but only just!

The first thing I had to do to it was to fill in several little cracks and holes with a quick-drying wood filler (see page 13). This was easily applied using the flexible blade of a palette knife.

When the filler had dried, I rubbed it down first with a medium-grade sandpaper and then with a fine one, before going over it with a tack rag to leave a smooth, dust-free surface (see page 13).

PAINTING THE SHELF
To mix this beautifully subtle colour, I squeezed about 2.5cm (1in) of Ultramarine designer colour into the bottom of a jam jar and added a little dot of Lemon Yellow. I mixed these together, and got a very bluey green to which I added just a touch of Raw Umber and a little water. I then gradually spooned in some white emulsion paint and mixed it into the colour until the shade began to look right.

As I wanted the shelf to look quite faded I also added a little more water until the paint was about the consistency of single cream.

Because the shelf was really a rough one to start with and had then been quite extensively filled, I had to give it a second coat of the emulsion mix after the first one had dried to cover up its worst features. If you are painting something in better condition, this colour looks lovely if you leave it slightly grainy with some of the pine showing through.

Book shelves are difficult to decorate from the point of view that the most interesting surfaces are normally covered in books and the ends are quite often obscured by being squashed up against a wall. Nevertheless I decided to decorate both ends of this book shelf in the hope that at least one of them would end up being visible and hedged my bets by trimming the edges in a comple-mentary colour.

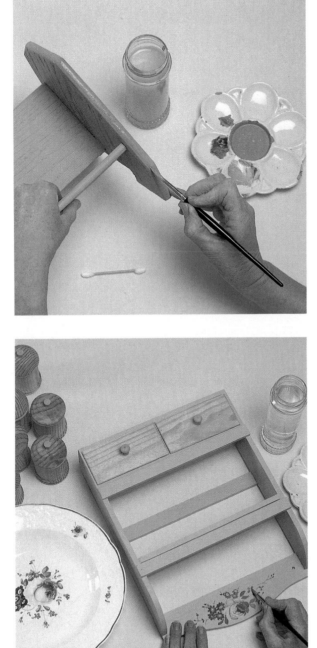

▶ **Painting the book shelf**
*After decorating the sides
of the book shelf, I then
painted the front edges in
the main colour.*

▶ **Painting the spice rack**
*I copied a pattern from a
china plate for the spice
rack, adapting the design
elements so they would fit
into the long, narrow
shape.*

FREEHAND DECORATION

I wanted the decoration on the shelf and the other pine pieces to look unsophisticated and spontaneous, so I intended to put the design on freehand with very little prior drawing. If you are skilled and confident enough to take freehand painting in your stride, there is no reason why you shouldn't paint directly onto the emulsion using either designer colours or acrylics. If you are not quite so sure, however, and feel the need for a safety net, it would be a good idea to give your shelf a coat of clear, matt polyurethane varnish at this point and paint your design on in acrylics when it is dry. Then if you do happen to make a mistake, you can easily wash the paint off without disturbing the base coat underneath. You will find that designer colours do not take so well on top of varnish and are easily moved by subsequent varnishing.

I intended to take the design from a plate as my inspiration and, in order to work out exactly how it was going to fit into the space at the end of the shelf, I first made some scale drawings on paper. When I found an arrangement that I liked, I lightly sketched a *few* basic guidelines onto the actual shelf and then copied the design from the plate freehand using simple brush strokes (see pages 36–7).

When I had decorated both ends of the shelf to my satisfaction (and, by the way, they do not have to be identical in every particular!) I chose one of the dominant colours and used it to trim the front edges of the shelf. I then allowed the paint to dry and gave the whole thing a final coat of clear, matt polyurethane varnish.

SPICE RACK

The little spice rack was in a much better condition than the shelf and only needed the lightest rub down with some fine sandpaper. Then I painted it with the same mixture as before except, because the grain was so attractive, I decided to leave some of the pine unpainted and therefore ignored the drawers and the pots apart from their knobs and a little trim around the tops.

I took the design from the same source and painted and varnished it in exactly the same way as for the shelf.

▶ **The spoon holder**
This pine spoon holder looked rather grubby and in desperate need of pretty decoration.

▶ **Planning a design**
I took the design for the spoon holder from an old plate and, although I intended to make a freehand copy, I took the precaution of planning it out on a piece of paper before I started.

▶ **Painting the design**
Most ceramics are painted with the same single brush-stroke technique as folk art, so it is relatively easy to adapt a design from a piece of china. Always try a few practice strokes on a piece of paper before you start though.

SPOON HOLDER

The spoon holder was a bit of a problem because it had obviously been well used and was very greasy and stained with what looked like ink.

Hot detergent, water and fine wire wool soon got rid of the grease and I finally shifted most of the ink with a cotton bud dipped in domestic bleach.

After this onslaught I wiped the whole thing with a lint-free rag, wrung out in cold water, and allowed it to dry.

If you have to clean something up in this way, try not to make the wood too wet in the process as this will lift the grain and give you a great deal of rubbing down to do.

When the spoon holder was dry, I did rub it down with some fine sandpaper and then painted it with two coats of the emulsion mixture, leaving a little of the pine showing so that it matched the spice rack.

I mapped out the design in the same way as I had for the shelf and painted and varnished it so that it matched the other two items.

◄**The revamped kitchen**
*Although pieces decorated
with folk art look
absolutely in their
element in this type of
rustic kitchen, they also
look surprisingly good in
more modern settings,
where they soften and add
charm to the severe lines.*

▲ The old iron pot
Although rusty and in need of repair, this pot was an ideal shape for barge painting.

Old Iron Pot

This pot was sold to me by a very dubious-looking gentleman, wearing a fez and sunglasses, at approximately 6.45 am. But in case you think I was enjoying some gloriously exotic holiday, I must tell you that he was also wearing a flying jacket, jeans, trainers and an earring.

No one said it was easy finding a bargain and I had gone to a famous race course where they hold an antique/junk market twice a month. It was winter and I had donned my warmest outfit and had joined the hundreds of other enthusiasts who regularly get up at the crack of dawn to stumble through the inevitable howling gales and driving rain while seeking out fabulous bargains. As is usual in the dark of winter, I was searching for mine with a hot cup of coffee in one hand and a flashlight in the other. It was a wonder that I still had the strength to barter when I finally found my pot – but I did!

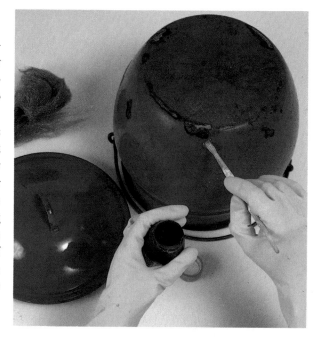

► Removing rust
Before you can burnish the rust-affected areas with wire wool, paint on rust remover and wait for it to do its work.

► Priming the pot
I gave the pot two coats of red oxide to protect it from any further attacks of rust.

MATERIALS
Rubber gloves
Rust remover
Fine wire wool
Waterproof abrasive paper (wet and dry)
Damp cloth
Red oxide
3 x 2·5cm (1in) house-painting brushes
Midnight Blue enamel paint (No.4 size)
Pencil & paper
Piece of chalk
Small pots of enamel paint in: Crimson, Bright Red, Yellow, White, Lime Green, Tan, Black
White spirit
Artist's brush size 3 (sable or synthetic mixture)
Polyurethane gloss varnish

REMOVING THE RUST
The first thing I had to do with the old pot was get rid of all the rust, which with modern rust removers and wire

wool is a surprisingly easy job – although it is essential to wear rubber gloves while you are doing it.

When I had indeed removed all the rust and those parts of the pot were *gleaming*, I rubbed down the rest of the paintwork with some waterproof abrasive paper until the whole thing was as smooth as possible. I then wiped it over with a damp cloth to get rid of any specks and allowed the pot to dry.

I gave the pot two coats of red oxide to protect it from any further outbreaks of rust and then rubbed it down lightly with very fine sandpaper before continuing as follows.

BARGE PAINTING DECORATION

I had decided to decorate this piece with the exuberant roses traditionally associated with narrow boats and so my next step was to paint the background with one of the coloured enamels most commonly used for this kind of painting. In theory, almost any of the enamel colours could be used for the background but, in practice, the darker colours seem to be the most popular and show the roses off to their greatest advantage.

I gave my pot two coats of Midnight Blue enamel, allowing the recommended drying time of six hours between each coat.

Traditionally the themes for canal boat decorations are limited to scenes with castles and groups of roses and daisies, but there is scope for plenty of variation within these limits in both the designs and the actual methods of painting. Obviously the swags of roses on my pot might not fit onto any project that you might wish to decorate, but the actual method of painting the flowers will remain the same and you can easily re-group them.

Before I started to apply the decoration to my pot, I worked out roughly the shape of my design on a piece of paper and then chalked circles onto the pot where the roses were going to appear.

There is no need to be mathematically perfect when it comes to executing one of these designs, because any discrepancies will only enhance the unsophisticated and lively look of true barge painting. Having said that, however, you must make sure that the base circles for the roses are far enough apart to allow for the petals and not so far apart that they look isolated. The same of course goes for the leaves and the daisies.

My next step was to paint in the circles and shadows for the roses (see page 36) on both the lid and the pot, using an artist's brush. While these were drying I carefully painted in the leaves and the centres for the daisies. When everything had dried, I continued by first putting the top petals on the roses and then by completing the daisies and putting in a few filling strokes, stamens and trimmings (see page 37).

I left the pot to dry overnight and then gave it a coat of varnish; I then left it for another 24 hours, before applying a final coat of varnish.

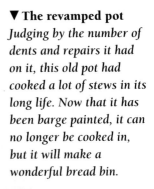

▼ **The revamped pot**
Judging by the number of dents and repairs it had on it, this old pot had cooked a lot of stews in its long life. Now that it has been barge painted, it can no longer be cooked in, but it will make a wonderful bread bin.

Barge Painting Colours

ROSES   **DAISIES**   **LEAVES**

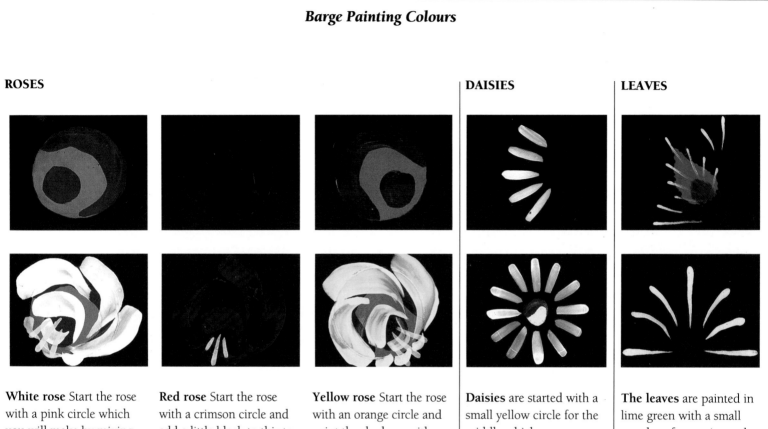

White rose Start the rose with a pink circle which you will make by mixing bright red and white together. Make the shadows with bright red and the top petals with white. The stamens are painted with yellow.

Red rose Start the rose with a crimson circle and add a little black to this to make the colour for the shadows. Paint the top petals with bright red and the stamens in yellow.

Yellow rose Start the rose with an orange circle and paint the shadows with crimson paint. Paint the top petals and the stamens in yellow.

Daisies are started with a small yellow circle for the middle which you may also encircle with some pale blue, but that is optional.

The yellow centre has a small bright red brush stroke flicked around one side and a circle of white petals around the outside.

The leaves are painted in lime green with a small smudge of tan paint at the base. The veins are painted in yellow.

All the filling lines and trimmings are usually painted in yellow, but you can intersperse another colour here and there.

1 Rose petal strokes
Paint the rose petals in this order: first the two central petals then, working from left to right, the three large outer petals, followed by the three smaller ones.

Apply the stamens last of all when the roses are completely dry.

Hold your brush upright and press it down so that half of it is flat against the surface. Then pull the brush towards you, lifting and curving it so that you finish the stroke with only the point touching.

2 Useful decorative stroke Hold your brush upright so that just the tip touches the surface. Then, moving from left to right and curving the line, dip the brush down and back up to finish on the tip again.

3 Daisy and border stroke Press the first quarter of the brush on to the surface and move the brush back, lifting it at the same time so that you finish on the tip.

4 Thin decorative stroke or stamens Press the tip of the brush onto the surface and pull it back fairly quickly, lifting it at the same time.

5 Small rose petal stroke Make in the same way as (1), using less of the brush and curving upwards.

6 Leaves Starting and finishing on the point of the brush, pull the brush towards you, flattening it while curving it out and in.

Start at the same point and make the second stroke in the same way, only curve out in the opposite direction.

Fill in the centre with one or two extra strokes.

Add the tan dot while the green leaf paint is still wet.

7 Long and curved decorative strokes These are made in the same way as (2), only your brush must be well charged with paint and you should lift the brush gradually as you move towards the point.

Key Holder

This little object which I am now calling a key holder used to hang in someone's hall with three clothes brushes hanging from its hooks. I don't know if we have all given up grooming or what, but you seldom see one performing its original function nowadays although they make wonderful hooks for hanging up dog leads and keys.

MATERIALS
Fine wire wool
Methylated spirits
Fine sandpaper
Tack rag
2 x 2·5cm (1in) house-painting brushes
Brunswick Green enamel paint (No.4 size)
Piece of chalk
Small pots of enamel paint in: Crimson, Bright Red, Yellow, White, Lime Green, Tan
Artist's brush size 3 (sable or synthetic mixture)
Polyurethane gloss varnish

► **The key holder**
Stripped of its brushes, this one-time brush holder was the perfect place to hang up keys in the kitchen.

► **Barge painting**
I made each petal in a single brush stroke, lifting the brush as I pulled it towards me.

I removed the mirror and hooks from the key holder and wiped the base with fine wire wool and methylated spirits to clean it. However, the varnish on the base came up so perfect and shiny that I also gave it a quick rub over with some fine sandpaper, to give it a slight 'key' so that the paint had a surface to cling to.

I decided to barge paint the key holder to match the old pot but, as the nature of this type of decoration is to look random, I gave it a different-coloured background and a slightly different pattern.

I went over the key holder with a tack rag to make sure that there wasn't any debris left from the wire wool and sandpaper. Then I gave it two coats of Brunswick Green enamel paint, leaving six hours between each coat.

After the last coat was dry, I painted and varnished the key holder in a similar way to the pot. Finally, I cleaned and replaced the mirror and treated the revamped key holder to three shiny, new brass hooks.

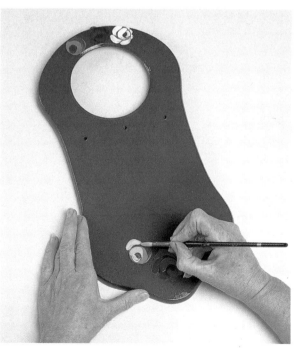

Butter Dish

I bought this round, wooden box because it looked like something I could renovate and because it was extremely cheap. However, I didn't have any particular idea what to do with it and was prepared to wait until inspiration struck and its moment of glory came. I was just walking away from the stall, however, when the woman behind it said, 'I'm sorry to see that go . . . my grandfather made it for me.'

From that moment on I felt obliged to do something meaningful with the box. The stallholder had a foreign accent and I immediately conjured up pictures of Heidi and her grandfather, green valleys and cows with cow bells.

That is why, even in these days of cholesterol watching, my wooden box became a king-sized butter dish with a cow on top.

MATERIALS
Fine sandpaper
Tack rag
Primer
2 x 4cm (1½in) house-painting brushes
Pale Yellow eggshell paint
Tracing paper
Pencil
Drawing pad
Tape measure
Acrylic paints
Artist's paintbrush
Clear, satin polyurethane varnish

The box was beautifully made from a smooth, hard wood and needed very little rubbing down before I tacked (see page 13) and then primed it.

When the primer was dry I gave it one coat of eggshell paint and left it to dry for 24 hours. Then I gave it two more coats of paint, leaving them for 24 hours between applications, and rubbing down and tacking the box each time.

◀ **The butter dish**
Outside junk fairs are full of small, inexpensive, wooden items like this, which are perfect for practising your decorative techniques on.

◀ **Designing the border**
I measured the circumference of the butter dish and divided this measurement into equal parts so that I could put alternate buttercups and daisies into each section. I then drew a strip the same length as the circumference and 4cm (1½in) deep on a piece of paper, and divided that up in a similar way.

DECORATING THE BUTTER DISH

While the box was drying I found a picture of a cow which happened to be the right size for the lid. If you find an illustration that either needs enlarging or reducing, take it to your local photocopying shop, where you can have it copied at the right size and even in colour if you want.

I traced the picture of the cow and transferred it onto the lid when the paint was quite dry (see page 61). Then, using the original picture as a guide, I painted her with acrylic paints.

The bottom half of the box also needed some kind of ornamentation and I decided to put a border of very simple buttercups and daisies around the top.

I drew a plain border 4cm (1½in) deep around the box and a similar strip, the same length as the circumference of the box, on a piece of paper.

I then measured around the circumference and divided that measurement into equal parts so that I could put alternate buttercups and daisies into each section.

Working on the paper, I divided the strip up into similarly equal parts and drew four alternate flowers with a couple of leaves and a bud to make it more flowing.

I traced this drawing including the outer edges of the strip and used it over and over again to transfer the drawing all around the border on the box.

When the border was complete, I painted it with acrylic paints and allowed a little time for the acrylics to dry before varnishing the outside only with clear, satin polyurethane varnish.

My intention is to find a glass liner for the box so that I do not have to wash the whole box whenever I put in fresh butter, but in the meantime the bottom of an ice-cream tub is doing the job.

The Dining Room

One of the assets of furnishing with junk is that you can usually afford to buy most of the furniture for one room at the same time and therefore make sure that it all tones and

matches. Thus the colours in the sideboard match the painting on the table, which picks up the tartan on the chairs, which in turn echoes the dark green of the bureau.

I wonder how many road accidents are directly related to the siren call of rubbish skips, left in the street outside houses. It seems almost wilfully irresponsible to top off your skip with such enticements as a beautiful 1930s sideboard or an elegant bureau, but that is exactly where both these pieces shown in this chapter came from *and* on separate occasions.

Coming upon such treasures when you least expect them does tend to make your driving dangerously erratic! But once you are safely parked and have calmed down your passenger and the man in the car behind, you will probably find, as I did, that the owners of the skips are only too glad to *give* you the items and will probably help you to your car with them!

▶ **The sideboard**
Because the sideboard was already very ornate, I planned to give it a simple colourwash to highlight the grain of the oak.

▶ **Painting details**
I painted the flowers with gouache paints so that I could keep the colours subtle and semi-transparent to match the colourwash.

Sideboard

Because the sideboard was already very decorative with its carved flowers and curved handles, I decided to keep any further decoration very low key. A cream colourwash provided just the right note and worked well with the grain of the oak. I also decided to add a little faded colour to echo the tartan on the table and chairs.

MATERIALS
Fine sandpaper
Tack rag
Cream emulsion paint
Old tablespoon
Jam jar
2 x 5cm (2in) house-painting brushes
Clean cloths
Designer colours (gouache)
Artist's paintbrush (sable or synthetic mixture)
Artist's 'liner' brush (synthetic)
Sanding sealer
Clear, matt polyurethane varnish

A colourwash of this kind should always be applied to stripped furniture so that the colour can penetrate the wood and display the beauty of the grain. As the sideboard was currently covered in varnish, the first job was to take it to the strippers (see page 20).

When the sideboard returned, I took the doors right off – they were halfway off anyway and it is a lot easier to deal with large pieces in bits if at all possible. I then rubbed it down thoroughly with fine sandpaper and went over it with a tack rag (see page 13).

COLOURWASHING THE SIDEBOARD
To make the colourwash, I spooned some of the cream emulsion into the jam jar with an old tablespoon and added sufficient water to bring it to a milky consistency.

I noted how many spoonfuls of emulsion and water I had used as I intended to treat most of the other furniture in the dining room in the same way. Although colourwash does go a surprisingly long way, it was likely that at some stage I would have to make some more and it would make it easier if I had a 'recipe' to refer to.

I sploshed a generous helping of the wash onto one end of the sideboard and brushed it out in the direction of the grain. Continuing in this way I completed both ends, the front, the top and the doors, in that order. I find that however adept you are at paint finishes, it is always a good idea to start with the parts that are least noticeable. Any discrepancies in colour, texture or technique usually become apparent at the beginning and if they really can't be cured and *must* be endured, then at least they are inconspicuous!

When I had allowed time for the paint to sink in and dry off a little (10 to 15 minutes), I went over the whole piece carefully with a soft, clean cloth, and rubbed the wash back to expose a little more of the grain.

When the paint was completely dry, I sanded the whole sideboard very lightly and tacked it.

PAINTED DECORATION

The dining room chairs were going to be upholstered in a tartan fabric and, although I wanted to echo this on the other pieces of furniture, the colours were much too strong and dark for the sideboard. I decided therefore to keep the colours the same, but alter the tone so they would appear faded and blend into the cream background in a much more subtle way.

To do this I mixed up designer colours to match the tartan and then diluted them with water. Using an artist's paintbrush, I painted the carved flowers and leaves with these designer colours so that they sank delicately into the wash. I noticed there was a narrow strip across the top of the doors that connected the two bunches of carved flowers; this seemed the ideal place to paint a length of faded tartan (see page 45).

The top of the sideboard looked a bit naked with all the detail on the doors and, as it had an edge very similar to that of the table, I decided to paint both with the

reddish/tan colour to make yet another unifying factor to the dining room suite. For this I used an artist's lining brush (see page 14).

When the designer colours were quite dry I gave the whole sideboard a coat of sanding sealer and allowed that to dry before finally applying a coat of clear, matt polyurethane varnish.

▲ Revamped sideboard
You can see the oak grain quite clearly through this lovely creamy colourwash. I have deliberately kept the colours of the tartan and flowers subtle so as not to lose the effect of softness.

▲ The table and chairs
Although the table and chairs were acquired on separate occasions, they looked good together because they came from the same period and had the same type of barley sugar legs.

Dining Room Table

This dining room table had obviously been put to very good use during the last fifty or so years and there were stains and small areas of missing and lifted veneer to be dealt with before the painting could begin.

MATERIALS
Small, flexible palette knife
Wood glue
Wood filler
Fine sandpaper
Tack rag
Cream colourwash (see page 42)
Clean cloths
2 x 5cm (2in) house-painting brushes
Small pieces of stiff card
Ruler
Pencil
Scissors
Designer colours (gouache)
Artist's paintbrush (sable or synthetic mixture)
Artist's lining brush (synthetic)
Sanding sealer
Clear, matt polyurethane varnish

PREPARING THE TABLE
Like the sideboard, the table had to be stripped before it could be worked upon and luckily all of the staining disappeared in the process. Unfortunately the veneer then lifted even more and had to be dealt with first before anything else could be done.

To replace the veneer, I loaded the thin end of a palette knife with plenty of quick-drying wood glue and slid it underneath and up and down the length of the loose piece, so that it was well coated. I then pressed the wood back in place with a damp cloth and removed all traces of excess glue. Finally I left it to dry, under the weight of an old-fashioned flat iron (a pile of heavy books would do just as well).

When the veneer repair was completely dry, I used the same flexible palette knife to fill the several little indentations where the veneer had disappeared completely, with a neutral-coloured wood filler (see page 13).

The wood filler dried fairly quickly and then I was able to give the table a complete rub down with fine sandpaper, although here and there, and especially on the barley sugar legs, there were still traces of varnish which needed wire wool or coarser sandpaper.

When the table was completely sanded, I gave it one final rub over with the tack rag to collect up all the debris and proceeded to colourwash it in the same way as the sideboard (see page 42).

APPLYING A TARTAN BAND

To pick up the tartan on the chairs (see page 46) I decided to give the table a broad band of faded tartan, running around about 5.5cm (2¼in) in from the edge of the table. To do this I prepared a piece of stiff card measuring approximately 7.5cm x 4cm (3in x 1½in).

I measured 5.5cm (2¼in) in from one end of this card and made a pencil mark approximately in the middle of the width. I then cut a V-shaped notch out of the end nearest to the pencil mark with its sides meeting in a point on the mark.

Holding this piece of card positioned with its un-notched end flush with the table edge, I moved it around the table making a pencil mark in the extreme point of the notch at regular intervals.

When I finally joined these dots I had an oval pencil line that ran around the table 5.5cm (2¼in) in from the edge.

As the band was going to be 2.5cm (1in) wide I prepared another card with a notch 8cm (3¼in) from the table edge and repeated the procedure. I divided this band up into sections approximately 4cm (1½in) long and, using an artist's paintbrush, I painted them alternately with faded blue and green.

To give the effect of the tartan that was on the chairs (see page 46), I took the long lining brush and ran a continuous reddish/brown line through the middle of the blocks of colour and parallel to the edge of the table (see page 14). Then, continuing with the same colour and using the lining brush again, I painted short lines across the middle of each of the blue sections at right angles to the first line.

All that was needed then to give the impression of tartan was a similar line, in white, across each of the green sections.

Finally I painted the extreme edge of the table to match the top of the sideboard. When the painted band was dry, I finished the table with a coat of sanding sealer and then a coat of matt varnish in a similar way to the sideboard.

◀ Colourwashing
When the table had been stripped and rubbed down I painted on the cream colourwash in generous strokes using a wide paintbrush.

◀ Painting on the tartan
Having measured out the tartan band, I began to fill in the main colour sections with very dilute gouache paint.

▶ **The revamped chairs**
As the dining chairs had the 'actual' tartan covering, I decided to content myself with merely colourwashing them to match the table and sideboard. Another option would have been to paint a few flowers across the backs, to match the ones on the sideboard.

Dining Room Chairs

These dining room chairs turned up quite uneventfully and extremely cheaply at a local auction. They were exactly what I wanted because, like the dining room table, they were made from oak and had barley sugar legs.

When I got them home they matched perfectly and, as the backs of the chairs were so plain, I was quite sure that I could easily make up the rest of the set (I had only bought two chairs).

Several months later I have become an authority on plain chair backs – there are many and they are extremely varied! I haven't found any to match mine yet, but in the meantime I am specializing in tête-à-têtes . . .

I had decided to upholster the chairs in a tartan fabric – I love the combination of dark blues and greens with a cream colourwash, but what really makes this work is that extra little hint of red in the tartan.

MATERIALS

TO PAINT THE CHAIRS

Fine sandpaper
Tack rag
Cream colourwash (see page 42)
2 x 5cm (2in) house-painting brushes
Clean cloths
Clear, matt polyurethane varnish

TO UPHOLSTER THE SEATS
(Covers four drop-in seats)

1–2m (40–80in) cotton felt wadding
Scissors
75cm (30in) calico, 1.75m (70in) wide
12mm (⅜in) fine tacks
Hammer (magnetic upholsterer's hammer if possible)
1.5m (60in) flame-resistant tartan fabric, 1.35m (54in) wide
75cm (30in) bottom cloth

▶ **Covering the seats**
When I came to the corners, I pulled the fabric down hard diagonally and tacked the fabric in position.

PREPARING THE CHAIRS

The chairs came back from the strippers in need of nothing more than a rub down with fine sandpaper and a dust with the tack rag.

After that they were colourwashed using the same colour as the sideboard (see page 42) and finally given a coat of matt varnish.

UPHOLSTERING THE SEATS

My chairs were still covered in the original material and, as it was quite sound, I decided to leave well alone and just plump the seats up with a little wadding.

Enquiries at my local upholsterer's produced all the necessary materials and I found that cotton felt wadding was appropriate for the job.

I cut this into pieces big enough to cover the top of each seat with just a little extra, so that it didn't stray down onto the sides, where it would eventually prevent the seats from fitting neatly into their holes.

The next job was to cut pieces of calico that were 7.5cm (3in) larger all around than the tops of the seats. These I

laid over the cotton felt wadding and, taking each seat in turn, I proceeded to tack the calico in place by first holding the seat so that it rested on its front edge while I put two or three holding tacks along its back edge. With these in place I could then smooth the calico across the top of the seat, pulling firmly against the back edge.

Laying the seat on its back I then gently pulled the fabric and put three holding tacks in each side, avoiding the corners. I completed the tacking on each side and removed the original holding tacks along the back edge.

Turning my attention at last to the corners, I pulled the fabric down hard diagonally and tacked the calico in position. I then folded the excess fabric back, still pulling firmly, and pleated it neatly on either side of the point. When I was quite sure that there were no wrinkles in the fabric I tacked the pleats in place.

I trimmed off the excess calico and repeated the process with the tartan, making sure when I tacked it that the lines were straight and that I didn't hit the previous line of tacks!

Finally, I cut pieces of bottom cloth approximately 2cm (¾in) larger than the base of the seats, folded the edges under and tacked them in position so that they covered all the previous tacking and gave a neat finish to the bottom of the chair.

I was very pleased with my chairs when I had finished them and, luckily, the upholstery side had been quite straightforward. However, if you are not very skilled in that direction and find yourself with a particularly tatty piece of upholstery, my advice is to leave it to the experts!

▲ The bureau
Although I am pretty sure that it is not that old, the lovely simple lines of this bureau are very reminiscent of the Arts and Crafts movement.

Bureau

Although I am pretty sure it is not that old, the lovely, simple lines of this oak bureau are very reminiscent of the Arts and Crafts movement. I have tried to retain that feeling by using a very simple stencil against a typically dark green colourwash.

The verdigris finish on the hinges and knob ties in well with the stencil and has made quite a feature of them in contrast to the rather shrinking violets they were before the decoration.

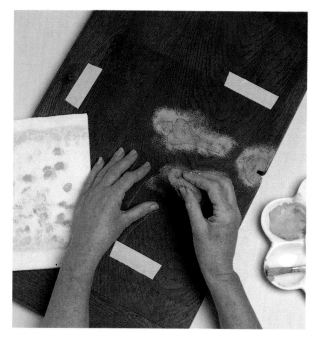

MATERIALS
Fine sandpaper
Tack rag
Dark Green emulsion paint
Jam jars
2 x 5cm (2in) house-painting brushes
Clean cloths
Tracing paper
Drawing paper & pencil
Technical drawing pen or fine felt pen
Masking tape
Plastic film for stencilling
Cutting mat
Craft knife
Stencil brush
Acrylic craft paint: Turquoise, Pale Blue
Old tablespoon
Emulsion paint: Dark Blue-green, Peppermint Green,
Pale Blue, Pale Turquoise
Methylated spirits
Sieve
Whiting
Several hog's-hair artist's
paintbrushes
PVA glue
Small, natural sponge
Clear, matt polyurethane varnish
Wax polish

Once again this piece had to be stripped before it could be colourwashed. I then removed the flap, mock hinges and knob before proceeding to rub it down with some fine sandpaper to smooth the surface and dust it over with the tack rag (see page 13).

Using the same process as for the sideboard (see page 42) I colourwashed the bureau in Dark Green and left it to dry while I tackled the stencil.

MAKING A STENCIL

I used the cut-out at the back of the bureau as my pattern and carefully copied it onto a piece of tracing paper so that I could use it as the basis of my stencil design. I also traced the very simple shape at the top of the hinge and, using this as a central point with the other shape repeated and radiating out around it, I designed and cut a stencil to go at the back and on the flap of the bureau (see page 70).

To make the stencil look similar in character to the verdigris, I applied the Turquoise and Pale Blue acrylics together, using a sponge. When the stencils were dry, I gave the bureau a coat of clear, matt polyurethane varnish. When this was dry, I gave the bureau several coats of wax polish to give it a dull sheen.

I gave the little knob and the hinges a verdigris finish (see page 85) and rubbed the hinges back well so that quite a lot of the copper colour was showing through. The verdigris was varnished with diluted PVA glue (see page 13) and allowed to dry before the whole thing was reassembled.

Picture Frames

What is it about interesting old picture frames? When you are desperately looking for something specific they disappear from the face of the earth, but when you couldn't care less if you never saw another one, they appear to breed in your garage!

None of this trio is particularly old but needless to say they were secondhand and extremely cheap.

◄ Sponging the stencil
To make the stencil look similar in character to the verdigris on the bureau, I applied the acrylics with a sponge, using both the turquoise and pale blue together.

◄ The revamped bureau
To a hoarder like me, it is hard to understand how anyone could abandon this handsome bureau and leave it lying on a skip, but that is where it was rescued from before a dark green colourwash, some stencilling and a verdigris finish on the hinges gave it a new lease of life.

CHEAP AND NASTY PLASTIC FRAME

You have to be careful about these frames. They come from China and are so cheap in the shops that you can actually pay more for them at a secondhand market and still go home thinking you have a bargain.

MATERIALS
Fairly coarse sandpaper
Damp rag
Dark Green emulsion paint
2 x 12mm (½in) house-painting brushes
25cm (10in) curtain lining
PVA glue or blind stiffener
Small, natural sponge
Pot of gold designer colour or poster paint
Clear, satin polyurethane spray varnish

These frames almost look like wood, but are in fact plastic, so the first thing I had to do with mine was to give it a brisk rub down with some fairly rough sandpaper, in order to give it a 'key' for the paint to cling to.

I then wiped it over with a damp rag to remove any dust and gave it two coats of the emulsion paint, allowing two or three hours' drying time in between.

When the second coat of emulsion paint was completely dry, I made a small bow with longish streamers using curtain lining (see page 80) and stiffened it with diluted PVA glue.

I arranged this in place on one side of the top of the frame and left it to dry.

When the bow was completely dry and stiff, I gave the whole frame, bow and all, two more coats of emulsion paint.

Providing you have already painted the object with a water-based paint like emulsion, gold designer colour is wonderful for sponging a little bit of glamour onto small items like this.

I sponged slightly diluted gold paint all over the frame and the bow (see page 82) and gave it a couple of thin coats of clear, satin spray varnish when it was dry.

▶ The 'bow' frame
When the fabric bow was completely dry and stiff, I gave the whole frame, bow and all, two more coats of emulsion paint.

▶ Spattering the frame
When I was quite sure that I had the spray well under control, I continued to spatter cream paint over the porphyry frame, until it was well covered and evenly distributed.

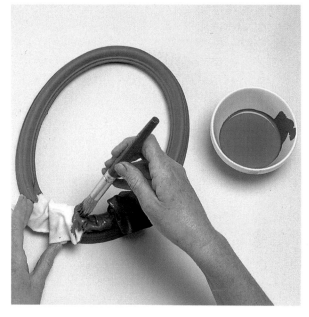

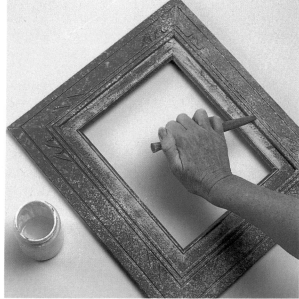

PORPHYRY FRAME WITH TARTAN INSET

Compared with the other two picture frames, this frame was always a winner from the start. It was wide enough to do something interesting with, in terms of decoration, and it had an inset and some carving to add to its attraction.

It also had an old price in foreign money written on the back of it which gave it a certain mysterious allure.

MATERIALS
White eggshell paint
2 x 4cm (1½in) house-painting brushes
Fine sandpaper
Tack rag
Artist's oil colours: Light Red, Yellow Ochre, Black
White spirit
Small, natural sponge
Gold bronzing powder
Stencil brush
Artist's acrylic varnish
Fine artist's paintbrush
Clear, satin polyurethane varnish

The frame, which was painted in an unforgettable green, was in excellent condition and only needed to be wiped over with a damp cloth before I gave it two coats of white eggshell paint. I left 24 hours between each coat and rubbed down and tack-ragged the frame after each one was dry.

I mixed a little of the white paint with some of the Light Red oil paint and added a little Yellow Ochre and a very small amount of Black to the mixture. When I had a light terracotta colour I added a *very* small amount of white spirit to this mixture and then sponged it all over the main part of the frame (see page 21).

I left this to dry for an hour or two until it had 'gone off' and was no longer shiny and then mixed a little of the Yellow Ochre and the white eggshell to make a cream colour. I thinned this to a milky consistency with some white spirit and then, taking up a little on the end of my stencil brush, I spattered some onto a spare piece of newspaper, by drawing my thumb across the tips of the bristles. I always do at least one trial spatter onto newspaper before I do it over the work, just to get rid of any lurking

blobs that might drip and ruin the effect.

When I was quite sure that I had the spray well under control, I continued to spatter over the frame until it was well covered and evenly distributed.

I left the cream spatter to dry for five or ten minutes and then I spattered on some diluted black oil paint, only this time I did it a little more sparsely.

After allowing the paint to dry thoroughly, I mixed a little of the gold bronzing powder with some acrylic varnish and spattered it lightly over the frame. I also used the gold mixture to pick out the indented lines around the frame and to paint the raised inner edge.

I left the frame to dry overnight and then gave it a coat of clear, satin polyurethane varnish.

I intended to hang the three frames in the dining room and as that was rapidly developing a tartan theme I had decided to make some tartan picture bows to display two of the frames on.

With this in mind I covered the inset with tartan ribbon which I was lucky enough to find in just the right width and in a similar tartan.

I mitred the corners (which might have proved tricky) by following the original mitring on the frame! I then glued the ribbon onto the frame with a glue gun, but any non-staining glue from a tube would have done.

VERDIGRIS METAL FRAME

I don't think anyone ever believed that this yellow metal frame was gold or even brass in its former life, but it looks much more valuable now that it is covered in verdigris (see page 85).

TARTAN PICTURE BOWS

MATERIALS
(Makes 2)
1m (40in) tartan fabric, 1·35m (54in) wide
Cotton
Pins
2 small, brass curtain rings

I arranged the fabric so that I could cut out:

4 Tails:
4 pieces each measuring 75cm x 15cm (30in x 6in)
2 Bows:
2 pieces each measuring 20cm x 30cm (8in x 12in)
2 Knots:
2 pieces each measuring 5cm x 15cm (2in x 6in)

I allowed 12mm (½in) for the seam allowance.

With the right sides together I folded the tails in half lengthwise and put a pin in the raw edges approximately 10cm (4in) from one end on each strip.

Starting at the end furthest from the pin I machined one of the strips until I came to the pin and then began to curve the stitching gently until it arrived at the folded corner.

I then trimmed the seam, turned the tail the right side out and pressed it so that the seam ran along one edge. I completed the other tails in the same way.

The little strips I also folded lengthwise and machined on three sides, before turning them the right side out and pressing them.

To make the bows, I folded the fabric lengthwise with the right sides together and put two pins in the raw edge so that each one was 5cm (2in) from the middle and so that it left a gap of 10cm (4in). I then machined up as far as the pin on both sides of the gap. I then folded the fabric so that the gap was in the middle of one side (rather than on the edge) and machined across each end. After trimming the seam I turned the strip inside out and pressed it. I neatly sewed up the gap by hand and then, bringing both ends of the bow into the middle on the same side as the gap, I slip-stitched them together.

Making sure that the slip-stitched seam was in the centre, I took the small strip and bound it around the middle of the bow to represent the knot. I then tucked in the raw edge and fastened it at the back.

I also tucked in the raw edges of the tails and sewed two of these and finally one of the brass curtain rings to the back of each bow.

The Living Room

I used shades of cream and yellow in the living room with the result that it looks beautifully sunny even on dull days. However, with such a light colour

on the sofa and chairs, I took the precaution of ordering extra fabric for cushion replacements and arm protectors.

I wanted to keep the living room light with a feeling of sunshine and decided to use creams and yellows.

I knew exactly the colour I wanted for the loose cover fabric, but when I went in search of it I found that the only way I could describe that particular shade of yellow was as a nearly-ripe banana. The base coat for the tables turned out to be a sort of lemon sorbet and the starting point for the tortoiseshell effect is definitely custard.

When I went to get the wall colour mixed, I tried hard to think of a description for the colour that didn't have gastronomic connotations. The shade cards were no help, but when I said that it was like the colour of creamed rice the paint man knew exactly what I meant and mixed it up perfectly. It was about then that I decided to go on a diet!

▶ **The armchair**
The suite was still very comfortable, but it was definitely beginning to look 'lived in'.

Three-piece Suite

I bought this three-piece suite secondhand when I was desperate for something to sit on in my living room.

It was advertised in the newspaper and I had been sitting on the floor for several weeks before I realized that the only way to get a good secondhand suite at a bargain price was actually to collect my local newspaper as it rolled off the presses.

By the time the newspaper boy delivered *my* paper, all the good suites had gone and their new owners, who were probably related to the newspaper boy anyway, were already plumping up the cushions.

As it was, even though I had personally collected the paper and phoned straightaway, I was told that this suite was already being held for another woman, who had gone to look for a van to move it in. The best I could do was be first in line should she fail in her mission.

I received a call from the seller's exasperated husband at 10 am. I could have the suite if I moved it *now*! All I had was an ancient Morris Minor and a very good friend, but

it was a beautiful bargain and we *did* move it.

As the suite was basically sound, I decided to make it some new loose covers.

MATERIALS
Drawing paper & pencil
Tape measure
Scissors
Pins
Dressmaker's chalk
30m (100ft) material, 1·35m (54in) wide (this included extra for arm protectors and replacing cushion covers)
Cotton
4m (4½yd) lining fabric
3 long zips for seat backs
10 zips for cushions

The main advice I can give you for undertaking a project like this is not to panic! Everyone will try to put you off making loose covers and indeed it does seem like a daunting task when you are contemplating it.

Once you get started, though, and provided you work your way through logically and put a label on everything you can stick a pin through, you will soon have a wonderfully revitalized three-piece suite.

MAKING LOOSE COVER PATTERN PIECES

The first thing I did was to work out how much fabric I needed. To do this I made a small sketch of the chairs and sofa and drew dividing lines where I could see that I would need a separate pattern piece. The main pattern pieces are as shown in the diagram opposite.

Measuring from top to bottom and from side to side at the widest points of each pattern piece on the actual chair, I came up with the measurements for a series of squares and rectangles from which each of the pieces could be cut.

I added 2.5cm (1in) to all these measurements to allow for 12mm (½in) seam allowances and 15cm (6in) for tuck-ins on all the relevant pieces – the back and bottom of the

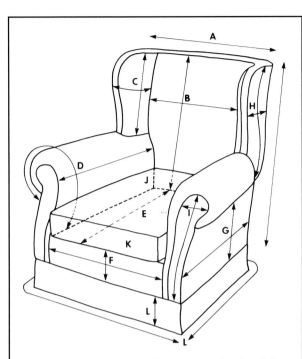

A   **Outside back** (the extreme back of the chair)

B   **Inside back** (from the top seam to the extreme edge of the tuck-in)

C   **Inside wing** (from the top seam to the arm of the chair)

D   **Inside arm** (from the tuck-in, up and over the arm, to just beyond the bulge)

E   **Seat** (from the seam with the front border to the extreme edge of the tuck-in)

F   **Front border** (the strip facing you at the front of the chair)

G   **Outside arm** (from the seam just under the bulge to the beginning of the frill)

H   **Outside wing** (from the top seam to the seam with outside arm)

I   **Arm scrolls** (curved fronts of arms)

J   **Cushions** (top and bottom rectangles)

K   **Cushion borders** (long strips that go around the cushions)

L   **Frill**

◄ **Measuring for covers**
Allow a 12mm (½in) seam allowance and 15cm (6in) for the 'tuck-in' when you are measuring the inside back, the inside arms and the seat for loose covers.

inside arms, the back and sides of the seat, and the bottom and sides of the inside back.

I then drew an open-ended rectangle onto a piece of drawing paper to represent a continuous piece of fabric. On this I drew each of the pattern pieces to scale so that I could see how they would fit and how much fabric I would need.

As my fabric had such a small design, I arranged my pieces fairly closely with all length measurements parallel to the vertical edges. If you are dealing with a larger design, you will need to take into account the pattern repeat and the fact that the main motif will need to be centred on the parts that show, such as the inside back.

To estimate the fabric for the frill, I measured the height from the bottom of the chair to the floor and added 5cm (2in) for hem and seam allowances. This gave me the depth of the frill pattern. For the length I measured the circumference and added half as much again. To get the exact dimensions of the cushion patterns I unpicked one back and one seat cushion and added the scaled-down dimensions of these pieces to my drawing.

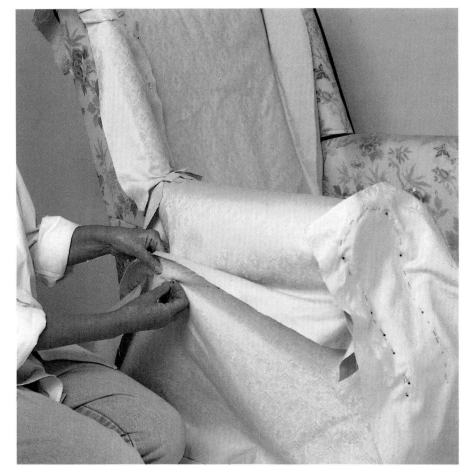

▲ Pinning fabric in place
To pin the outside arm to the arm scroll, I pinned the large rectangles together, moulding the fabric to the chair and easing it into two or three evenly-spaced pleats around the wing.

I could see that I had quite a lot of spare material available to cover the piping cord but, as I had ten cushions to pipe, I added another metre (40in) to be on the safe side.

When I had all the pieces plus the extra metre (40in) laid out on my plan, it was easy to estimate the total quantity of fabric needed. To estimate the piping cord I simply had to measure around the top and bottom of one cushion and multiply by ten. I labelled all the pieces on my drawing and then began to cut out all the actual rectangles, in their correct size, from the material, remembering to cut a lining for the frill out of the lining material. I also pinned a label to each of these pieces as I cut them out.

PINNING FABRIC IN POSITION

I measured and found the centre of each of the large areas on one of the chairs and marked it with chalk. I did the same with the corresponding pattern pieces so that when I eventually placed them on the chair the two chalk lines would be together. With the fabric right side out I pinned the outside back section of the cover in place, taking care to match the chalked lines and ensuring that all the seam allowances extended beyond the chair.

I put a few pins along the chalk line and then smoothed the fabric out towards the edges where I carefully put pins along the original seams of the old upholstery. By putting the pins in at right angles I found that it was possible to chalk over the pins so that I could locate the seam lines when the pieces were eventually removed for sewing.

I attached the front back, seat and front border in the same way, pinning seam allowances together to make a good fit at the top of the back and the front of the seat. I pinned the tuck-ins with a 12mm (½in) seam allowance and laid them on the seat of the chair.

I attached the wing and arm pieces for one side in a similar way, moulding the fabric to the chair and easing it into two or three evenly-spaced pleats around the wing. I tapered the tuck-in between the inside back and the inside arm from nothing at the top to the full allowance at the bottom.

When I was quite happy with the fit of everything, I went over the pins with dressmaker's chalk, as before, and then trimmed off all the excess fabric, leaving a 12mm (½in) seam allowance on all pieces (with the exception of the tuck-ins).

Here and there, and particularly on the curves and on the seam between the arm and the outside side, I cut some small notches in both sides of the seam allowances so that I could match them later.

SEWING THE CHAIR COVERS

I unpinned all the pieces and used the shaped pieces for the wing and arm as patterns for the other arm and wing by placing them with right sides together on a fresh piece of fabric. I then pinned and sewed the original arm and wing pieces together, matching the chalk lines and notches and with right sides together. I cut a few more notches in the curved seams to help with the fit and tried these pieces back on the chair.

I am glad to say that they fitted perfectly and I was then able to use the remaining arm and wing pieces as patterns for the other chair and the sofa, which of course were identical in that respect.

This done, I made up the remaining wing and arm for the first chair. Omitting all but the first 12.5cm (6in) of the vertical seam on the left outside back, I sewed the main seams on the back, seat and front border and attached the wings and arms on both sides, matching chalk lines and notches where necessary.

MAKING THE FRILL

The frill and its lining had been cut out in strips and I now sewed these together, allowing a 12mm (½in) seam allowance on both the frill and the lining. I pressed these seams flat and then, with right sides together, I pinned the fabric to the lining along one of the longer sides.

I pressed open this seam and then with the wrong side still facing, I turned up a 2.5cm (1in) hem of the main fabric on the side that was attached to the lining and sewed both the short end seams together. I then turned the whole strip right side out and trimmed off the excess lining fabric.

To gather the frill, I divided the strip into four equal parts and marked each section with a pin. Then, using the gathering stitch on my machine (or you can do it by hand) I gathered up each section separately and evenly, so that each one measured the same as one of the sides of the chair.

When the frill was completely gathered and reached right round the chair, I machined it to the bottom of the cover, starting and finishing at the opening for the zip. I then inserted the zip (see page 58) and pressed the fabric neatly to finish.

The second chair was completed in a similar way, as were the arms and wings of the sofa.

MAKING THE SOFA COVERS

As the sofa was so much wider than the chairs I had to add extra strips to the width of the material before I could cut the outside back, inside back, seat and front border.

To do this I measured the depth of the outside back from the seam line to the beginning of the frill and then added a 2.5cm (1in) seam allowance to this measurement.

I cut two pieces of fabric this depth by the whole fabric width. With right sides together I sewed them from top to bottom on either side. I then cut this tube of fabric down the middle of one side, parallel to the seams, and opened it out.

▲ Inserting the zip
I cut the back border for each cushion cover in two lengthwise and turned under and pressed back one long edge on each piece. Then I pinned each pair onto a zip so that the turned-under edges butted together over the teeth of the zip.

I made similar pieces for the other wide areas and then fitted them to the sofa and attached them to the other pattern pieces in the same way as the chairs.

The frill was made in the same way except that it was divided into three along the front and back for gathering.

MAKING THE CUSHIONS

To make the cushions I used the unpicked pieces of the old cushion cover as a pattern and cut out ten sets of new pieces. I also covered sufficient piping cord to go around each cushion twice (see page 91).

The back border for each cushion was slightly longer and wider than the front border and it was also cut in two lengthwise, so that it could accommodate a zip. I took each of these back pieces and turned under and pressed one long edge on each half of every pair. I then pinned each pair onto a zip, so that the turned-under edges butted together over the teeth of the zip, and machined them in place.

Allocating two lengths of covered piping to each cushion, I pinned and then sewed them onto the top and bottom pieces of each cushion (see page 91).

I then seamed the pieces of border together for each cushion and, making sure that the centre of the zip border corresponded with the centres of the top and bottom pieces, I machined first the top and then the bottom to the border. Before I turned the cushions out the right way again, I clipped and notched the corners.

Finally, and I have to admit with a sigh of relief, I sewed the zip into the back of the sofa and fitted my lovely new covers onto my tatty old suite.

Oak Chest

Nothing came cheaper than this piece of furniture, which was given to me by my mother when she moved house. For the sake of family harmony I should mention that it certainly did *not* qualify as junk!

It had been knocked about a bit though, and it did come from a time when thick, brown varnish was 'in'.

▲ The oak chest
The oak chest was panelled and had some linen fold carving, which was all but obscured by its heavy dark varnish.

MATERIALS
Fine sandpaper
Sanding sealer
4cm (1½in) house-painting brush
Wire brush
Liming wax
Fine wire wool
Soft cloths
Beeswax polish

When the chest returned from the strippers with all its lovely oak grain liberated at last from the varnish, I was loathe to cover it up again, and decided instead to emphasize the grain with liming wax.

I started by giving the chest a light rub down with fine sandpaper and followed this with a coat of sanding sealer. When the sealer was dry I opened up the grain on the chest by going over it firmly with a wire brush, working in the same direction as the grain. I used the wire brush over the whole chest, keeping an even pressure on the brush the whole time.

Then, taking some of the liming wax on a wad of wire wool, I rubbed it into the grain of the wood, first working against the grain and then working with it. I allowed a little time for the wax to dry and then, with a smooth wad of clean cloth and a little beeswax polish, I buffed up the whole chest. Next day I applied a thin film of beeswax polish to the surface and left this to dry for five minutes before buffing it off with a soft cloth. To get a harder surface and a beautifully deep shine, I still continue to beeswax the chest from time to time.

► Opening the grain
Using a wire brush, I pressed down firmly on the chest and made long, firm strokes, in the same direction as the grain, to open up the texture.

► Waxing the chest
Using a soft cloth, I rubbed liming wax into the chest to emphasize the grain. Subsequent waxing of the chest with beeswax will give it a hard surface and a deep, glowing sheen.

Nest of Tables

I think that a repetitive design on a nest of tables makes an unusually attractive item out of what is undoubtedly a very practical piece of furniture. Handpainting furniture does not require great artistic skill – patience and concentration are often more important.

Many people baulk at the idea of handpainting a design on a set of small tables, on the grounds that although painting one successfully might be possible, painting a second one to match could be distinctly risky, while painting a third would be pushing one's luck to the extreme.

Luck, however, has nothing to do with it and once you have made your design for the largest table, nothing could be easier than copying it onto the other two.

MATERIALS
Wood filler
Palette knife
Fine sandpaper
Tack rag
2 x 4cm (1½in) house-painting brushes
Primer
Pale Yellow eggshell paint
Artist's oil colours: Yellow Ochre, Raw Umber
Jam jar
White spirit
Old tablespoon
Natural sponge
Clear, satin polyurethane varnish
Drawing paper & pencil
Tracing paper
Ruler
Soft pencil
Masking tape
Ballpoint pen
Artist's paintbrush
Acrylic craft paints
Candle

▲ The nest of tables
I searched my old haunts a long time before I found these tables. They were a bit battered and had the glass missing from the top, but they were just what I wanted.

▶ Varnishing the tables
As the tables were bound to get a lot of wear and tear, I gave them a coat of oil-based polyurethane varnish. This also made it easier to rub off any mistakes when it came to putting on the ribbon border.

These tables were decidedly bashed-about when I bought them but, as I had been searching for just the right set for at least two years, I was very happy to have them.

Like many other things that are covered in broken varnish, they came back from the strippers looking much better than when they went.

My first task was to repair a small amount of damage to the moulding on the edge of the smallest two tables. This was easily put right by applying some wood filler using a palette knife with a thin, flexible blade.

When the wood filler had dried, I lightly rubbed down the repaired patch and the rest of the tables with some fine sandpaper, before dusting them all with the tack rag.

PAINTING THE TABLES
As the tables had been to the strippers and were very porous, I gave them all a coat of primer, which I allowed to dry before giving them a coat of yellow eggshell.

I left the eggshell paint to dry for 24 hours and then lightly rubbed it down and tacked it again. The tables needed two more coats of paint and I rubbed down and tacked after each one.

I intended to sponge the tables with a slightly darker yellow and to make this I put some Yellow Ochre oil paint into a jam jar and added a much smaller amount of Raw Umber. I mixed this to a creamy consistency with a little white spirit. I then stirred in some of the eggshell paint until the jam jar was about one-quarter full. I smeared a little of this mix onto the dry table-top to see if the colour was dark enough and, when I was satisfied, I added a similar amount of white spirit to the mix, so that the jam jar was now half-full of paint glaze.

I cleaned the experimental paint smear from the table with a turps-soaked cloth and, turning one of the tables upside down, I applied glaze to the legs and sponged it off (see page 21) with the natural sponge. I then turned the table up the right way again and completed the top in the same way.

I sponged the other tables similarly and left them to dry for 24 hours, before giving them all a coat of varnish.

DECORATING THE TABLES

I had decided to decorate the tables with a border of very stylized ribbon and a bow, which I had found on some Victorian tiles.

I measured the top of the largest of the tables and drew its proportions onto a large sheet of paper. I then drew a similar shape 6.5cm (2½in) in from the first, to mark the position of the border.

The design was so simple that it was possible to copy it freehand and I drew the winding strips of ribbon over the border line, twisting it symmetrically as it turned each of the four corners.

I marked the position for the bow halfway across the border at the front of the table and, still using the old tiles as my model, I drew it in line with the ribbon.

When I had completed the border design for the largest table, I taped a piece of tracing paper over the top of it and took a tracing.

Using this tracing I measured along the longest sides of the border and made a mark halfway along each side. I then joined these with a pencil line that stretched across the centre of the drawing. I repeated this exercise with the shorter sides so that the two pencil lines crossed at right angles in the middle.

Taking a soft pencil I repeated this on the table-top. Using the same soft pencil, I scribbled all along the border on the *back* of the tracing paper. Then, placing the paper scribbled-side down, I taped the tracing to the top of the table so that the crossed lines on the drawing matched up with those on the table-top, thus ensuring that the border was straight!

I carefully went over the drawing on the tracing paper with a red ballpoint pen so that I could see where I had been and so that the graphite which I had scribbled onto the back of the drawing would accurately transfer the design to the table. It was now relatively easy, by still using the Victorian design as my guide, to paint the ribbon and bow with acrylic paints.

To prepare the same design for the two smaller tables I reduced the size of the outer border, that is the distance

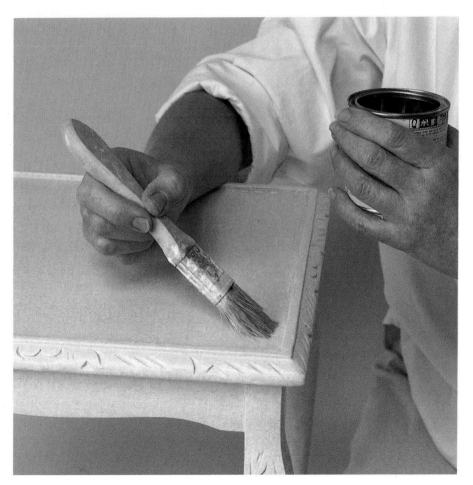

◄ Rubbing down
Using long, firm strokes and going with the grain, I rubbed the table-tops down with some fine sandpaper wrapped around a cork block.

► Sponging the table legs
I painted on the glaze and sponged it off with a natural sponge.

Once I had made the modified drawing I finished the smallest table in the usual way and then varnished all three tables.

My tables actually had insets for taking a sheet of glass in the top of them and I had a piece cut for each as an added protection. For tables that don't have this feature, an extra coat of varnish is advisable.

The tables were now ready to stack together again but, before I slid them into their places, I took a candle and rubbed it along the runners and the sides of the tables so that they would run smoothly and reduce the risk of chipping the paint.

Plant Stand

This plant stand was definitely past its first flush of youth when I bought it and was well qualified to be termed 'junk'.

As I didn't think I would ever completely iron out all its problems, I decided to give it a rough texture which would disguise the ones I could do nothing about. 'Bagging' the plant stand with an old plastic carrier bag not only fitted the bill, but seemed somehow appropriate for such a disreputable old thing.

MATERIALS
Wood filler
Palette knife
Fine sandpaper
Tack rag
Primer
Pale Yellow eggshell paint
2 x 4cm (1½in) house-painting brushes
Artist's oil paints: Yellow Ochre, Black
Jam jar
White spirit
Ruler
Pencil
Paper
Scissors

▲ The revamped tables
With their smooth painted surfaces and new glass tops, these tables are scarcely recognizable as being the original chipped nest of tables.

between the table edge and the painted border, by 12mm (½in) on each table. I then continued in the same way for the second size using my original tracing for the corners and the bow and filling in the slightly shorter sides freehand as before. I did all this on a sheet of drawing paper and proceeded to trace it, transfer it to the table and paint it, as for the larger table.

The smaller table was a little different and after I had established the outside edge of the table and the position of the border on a sheet of drawing paper, I had to copy the design freehand because the actual ribbon needed to be slightly thinner to keep the design in scale.

Masking tape
Plastic carrier bag
Stiff decorator's brush (for stippling)
Artist's paintbrush
Dark Green acrylic paint
Clear, satin polyurethane varnish

The plant stand was *so* disreputable that it had lost any varnish it might have had and didn't even need stripping.

It did need plenty of wood filler, though, before I primed it and gave it three base coats of yellow eggshell paint in a similar way to the nest of tables (see page 60).

I then made a paint glaze by mixing in a jam jar a very small amount of Black oil paint with a good squeeze of Yellow Ochre; I then added white spirit and eggshell paint as before (see page 60).

Most of the plant stand's 'figure faults' were on its legs so I intended to 'bag' those and the edge of the top tier. To give some contrast I was going to stipple the middle of the top tier and all of the bottom one.

I measured a border 5cm (2in) in from the edge of the top tier and drew it in with a pencil. I then cut a square of paper, slightly smaller than the one in the middle of the top tier, and used this to mask off the centre.

I taped the paper down with masking tape, making sure that the tape ran straight along the pencilled lines on the plant stand.

'BAGGING' THE GLAZE

Turning the plant stand upside down, I painted glaze on the legs and proceeded to pounce the bunched-up plastic bag into the glaze until the legs were all heavily textured with the tight, angular design.

I used a supermarket-type carrier bag, but you can use thicker, better-quality bags for a much more definite and broader design, while the soft, delicatessen-type bags will give a less defined effect.

I turned the plant stand up the right way and, taking the glaze slightly over the edge of the mask, I glazed the top and sides, before attacking the glaze once more with

▲ The plant stand
The plant stand was no beauty, but it was one of those useful pieces of furniture which fits in anywhere.

▶ Rubbing down
After filling in the numerous holes in the plant stand, I rubbed down the whole thing back to bare wood.

▶ Painting on primer
I painted the plant stand with primer to make it less porous and to seal the filler.

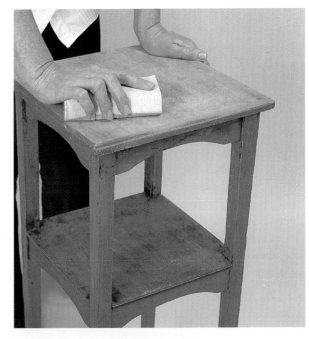

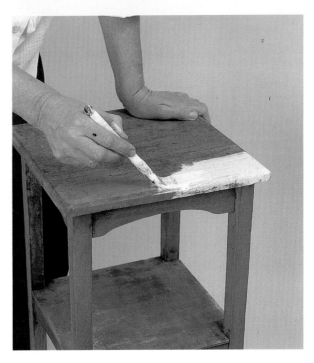

▶ Bagging
I painted on the glaze and went over it with a scrunched-up plastic bag to avoid too regular a pattern.

▼ Revamped plant stand
The plant stand had so many problems that only a fairly coarse paint finish was going to hide them. So from being a real 'plain Jane', it ended up being bagged, stippled and lined!

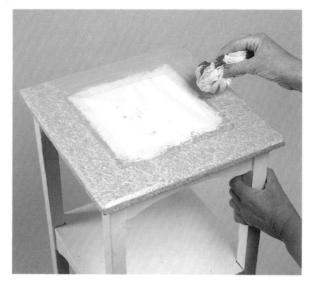

a fresh piece of bag, bunched as before.

I kept the remainder of the glaze in a screw-top jam jar and gave the bagging a couple of days to dry thoroughly before I removed the masking tape and paper.

I now needed to put masking tape on the other side of the pencilled line so that I could apply glaze to the centre square. However, because glaze is more fragile than paint at full strength, I took the precaution of sticking each strip of tape to my jeans to remove some of the adhesive before sticking it on the plant stand.

STIPPLING DECORATION
With the masking tape in position, I carefully painted glaze onto the middle section and also onto the bottom tier. Then, holding the decorator's brush with its bristles pointing downwards, I pounced it all over the glaze, making a very fine texture consisting of hundreds of tiny dots. I gave the glaze about 30 minutes to dry slightly and then carefully removed the masking tape.

When the glaze was quite dry I measured and drew a 12mm (½in) wide border over the join between the two textures and a similar border 7·5cm (3in) in from the edge of the bottom tier.

Using an artist's paintbrush and some Dark Green acrylic paint, I carefully painted this in and allowed it to dry before giving the whole plant stand a coat of varnish.

When the transformation was complete I'm sure the poor old thing thought it had died and gone to heaven!

Lamp Base & Shade

Little items, such as this beautifully turned wooden lamp base, can often be picked up in charity shops, which is where this one came from.

The lampshade, I hardly dare tell you, was new. Well, I am sorry, but lampshades like this one do not mature into junk very gracefully. They get irreparably dented and twisted and usually need the services of a soldering iron at the very least. It's much better to go out and buy a new one . . . at a cut-price store of course!

MATERIALS

Fine sandpaper
Tack rag
Primer
2 x 4cm (1½in) house-painting brushes
Warm, Light Yellow eggshell paint
Artist's oil paints: Raw Umber, Burnt Sienna, Light
Red and Black
Transparent oil glaze
Palette or old plate
Artist's paintbrushes
White spirit
Palette knife
Softener brush (see page 14)
Gold bronzing powder
Acrylic varnish
Mid-sheen, clear, satin polyurethane varnish

There are many wonderful ways of using varnishes to make a tortoiseshell effect which are almost indistinguishable from the real thing. This method, however, is blatantly faux, but it is great fun to do and gives a smart new finish to the elderly base and the brand new lampshade.

I stripped the lamp base myself (see page 20) and, when it had dried out, I gave it a rub down with fine sandpaper and dusted it with a tack rag, before giving it and the lampshade a coat of primer.

When the primer was dry I gave the shade and the base three coats of the eggshell paint, leaving 24 hours between coats and rubbing down lightly and tacking after each application.

FAUX TORTOISESHELL FINISH

I was intending to give the lamp four different-coloured glazes (see page 17) but, as the amounts used were going to be so small, it was easier to mix them on my palette rather than in separate jars.

Accordingly I laid out a small amount of each of the oil paints and a tablespoonful of transparent oil glaze on my

▲ The lamp base
The lamp base was beautifully turned and had a fascinating, red bakelite switch, but it was also covered in layers and layers of 'that' green which seems to turn up on everything.

◄ Applying the glaze
I dabbed on the light red glaze, fairly sparingly in little groups of two or three brush strokes.

◄ Softening the glaze
When all the glazes were in place, I took the softener brush and, using it very gently so that it only just touched the glaze, I brushed up and down the diagonals.

palette. I always use a glass palette, but you may use a more conventional wooden palette, a paper one or even an old plate if you prefer.

Using an artist's paintbrush, I mixed a little of the Raw Umber oil paint with a small amount of the white spirit to soften it, and then added some of the transparent oil glaze with my palette knife. When this mixture was well integrated, I added a few drops more of white spirit so that I had a glaze about the consistency of milk.

APPLYING THE GLAZES

Taking one of the larger brushes, I painted this glaze onto the shade in random squiggly lines which moved in a diagonal direction and left patches of the base colour still showing through.

I made the other oil paints into little pools of glaze in a similar way and took up some of the Burnt Sienna glaze on a fresh brush. I applied this along the same diagonals, but in separate, broad, curly strokes. I dabbed on the light red glaze sparingly in little groups of two or three brush strokes. I also used the black glaze sparingly and painted it on in little groups of curly, comma-shaped brush strokes. Then, using the softener brush, I brushed the glaze very gently up and down the diagonals, only just allowing the brush to touch the glaze. Then, imagining another set of diagonals going in the other direction, I lightly brushed up and down these invisible lines until the colours began to merge softly. Leaving the shade to dry, I painted the lamp base in the same way.

TRIMMING WITH GOLD

I left the lamp to dry for 24 hours and then mixed some of the gold bronzing powder into a little acrylic varnish.

I painted this mixture around the top and bottom binding of the lampshade and picked out some of the moulding on the lamp base. I rather like the rich effect of gold on tortoiseshell, but you might like to try a dark brown or even a white trim. When the gold was quite dry I gave the whole thing a coat of satin varnish.

The Bedroom

In its junk state the bedroom furniture looked like a very unlikely room set, but by using the same colours and fabrics and by

continuing the theme of roses throughout, the pieces now look as though they were made for each other.

Roses are a favourite theme of mine and I have thoroughly indulged myself with this bedroom furniture.

Luckily the bedroom is large enough to withstand such a riot of floribundas, but room size is something which you should take into account if you are repeating such a strong pattern on your furniture. Likewise I have kept to smaller pieces of furniture as this profusion of roses would be quite overwhelming if I'd included it on my wardrobes too.

Other items for the bedroom which you will find in abundance at junk fairs are bedside lamps and tables, pretty rugs, and a wonderful assortment of dressing table ornaments. If you really want to go to town you will even be able to find enough scraps of material to make a patchwork quilt for your bed, a project I am still considering. . .

▶ **The headboard**
The pine headboard already had a sound and unbroken coat of varnish when I bought it and only needed to be cleaned with fine wire wool and methylated spirits.

▶ **Cutting out roses**
Having found some wrapping paper with just the right kind of old-fashioned roses on it, I used large scissors to cut out the main pieces and then some very sharp, curved nail scissors to cut carefully around each flower and leaf.

▶ **Arranging the design**
When I had cut out several sets of flowers and leaves, I began to arrange the design on the headboard, using Blu-Tack as an adhesive so that I could take the pieces off and move them around until I was quite satisfied with the design.

Headboard

Sometimes, in company with a group of friends, I go out on a sort of bargain hunters' safari, to the type of open-air junk market that entails getting up in the small hours of Sunday morning.

On these occasions, while most reasonable people are still warm in their beds, we go out to hunt down specific items. This means that, apart from the statutory tape measure and plastic bag, we each carry a composite hit-list of each other's targets as we spread out and comb the area for bargains.

On the morning we found the long sought-after pine headboard I swear that each one of us had independently seen and made a bid for it before dawn broke, but amazingly we were all too late . . . it had been sold *and* for next to nothing!

When I got home, however, there it was in the porch . . . left by a kind but insomniac friend.

MATERIALS
Methylated spirits
Fine wire wool
2 or 3 x 4cm (1½in) house-painting brushes
Cream eggshell paint
Fine sandpaper
Tack rag
3 sheets of flowery wrapping paper

Curved nail scissors or craft knife
Blu-Tack
PVA glue
Small rubber roller
Clean lint-free cloth
Clear, matt polyurethane varnish
Crackle glaze
Artist's oil paint: Burnt Umber, Jet Black
White spirit
Jam jar
Old nylon stockings or tights

The varnish on the headboard was in good condition and only needed rubbing down with methylated spirits and wire wool to remove any polish or grease.

I followed this with three layers of cream eggshell paint, leaving 24 hours and rubbing down between each coat.

APPLYING DÉCOUPAGE DECORATION
While the paint was drying I got on with cutting out the roses, convolvulus and forget-me-nots from the sheets of wrapping paper.

I used curved nail scissors but you may prefer to use a sharp craft knife and cutting mat. Either way it is easier and safer if you cut the main outlines and shapes first and leave the small, delicate areas, such as stems and tendrils, until last.

When the last coat of paint was dry, I rubbed it down lightly and went over it with a tack rag. I then began to arrange the paper cut-outs on the headboard by sticking them on temporarily with Blu-Tack until I was sure that the design was pleasing and well balanced.

When I was happy with the design, I took each piece off in turn and painted the back of it with PVA glue before returning it to its position on the headboard.

I then went over it with a small rubber roller to make sure that all the surplus glue was squeezed out and that the paper was smooth and wrinkle-free. To make doubly sure of this and to mop up the excess glue, I went over the piece again with a warm damp cloth and rubbed around

the edges with the tip of a clean finger. Finally, I went carefully over the whole piece again, checking that there were no corners or edges coming un-stuck.

VARNISHING

I left the decorated headboard to dry for some hours and then gave it two coats of varnish, leaving 24 hours between each application.

Using fine sandpaper, I lightly rubbed down and tacked the second coat before applying four more coats, which I also rubbed down and tacked after each one had dried. Make sure that you only rub down very lightly when you are covering an item with découpage. It is very easy to go through the layers of varnish and ruin the paper cut-outs if you rub down too enthusiastically.

When the sixth layer of varnish had dried, I gave the headboard an application of antiqued crackle varnish (see page 24) which I allowed to dry before applying one last coat of matt polyurethane varnish.

▲ The revamped headboard
These lovely old roses were perfect for this headboard, which became more and more mellow as I added layer upon layer of varnish. A final treatment with crackle varnish completed the effect and made the headboard look really antique.

▶ **Cutting the stencil**
Using a sharp craft knife and cutting as evenly and accurately as possible, I began to cut out my stencil. I kept turning the stencil all the time so that I could ensure that I always cut towards myself.

▼ **The bedroom chair**
I loved the proportions of this chair but, as I intended to paint it in a very light cream, I wished it had been any other colour but black!

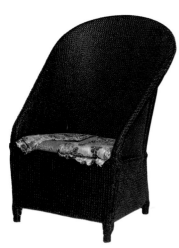

Bedroom Chair

This little chair is covered in the kind of weave which you often see mistakenly labelled as Lloyd Loom.

Try as I might, I cannot discover what its real name is, but I do know that its much smoother surface is far more amenable to stencilling than the genuine article.

MATERIALS
Oil-based spray paint
Tape measure
Drawing paper & pencil
Tracing paper
Technical drawing pen or fine felt pen
Masking tape
Plastic film for stencilling
Cutting mat
Craft knife
Acrylic craft paints
Stencil brush
Scissors
50cm (20in) cotton felt wadding
50cm (20in) patterned fabric
10mm (⅜in) fine tacks
Small hammer
50cm (20in) fine canvas

Unfortunately the chair had been smothered in black paint by the time I got to it, and the paint had been painted on rather than sprayed, so that most of the little holes in the weave were completely clogged up.

If you have the luck to find something in this weave which is still in its original state, it will look a lot better if you spray-paint it or even if you brush on several diluted coats of paint, rather than if you brush on two or three layers straight from the tin. Although this chair had already been spoiled from that point of view, I used spray paint on it anyway because I wanted the colour to match that of the ottoman and it took several applications of the cream paint to cover the black successfully!

DESIGNING & CUTTING THE STENCIL

I had already decided that the seat was going to be covered in the same fabric as the ottoman cover and the dressing table curtains and I wanted to design a stencil that used some of the main elements in this material. The stencil was also going to be used for the ottoman. I measured the area that I wanted it to occupy on the chair and found that the same-sized stencil would also fit well onto the front of the ottoman. I drew a shape on a piece of paper a little larger than the size I wanted the finished stencil to be and began to draw the design within the shape.

I copied one or two of the roses from the fabric onto my drawing pad, simplifying the shapes so that they would translate well into a stencil design. I added a few leaves and used some of the spiky blue flowers and an additional rosebud to balance the design.

If you have not made a stencil before, look at some of the commercially made stencils before you start and note how the design elements are held together by 'bridges' or 'ties' of the plastic film. These are the most vulnerable parts of your stencil, so try not to make them too delicate or they might twist or even tear.

I taped a piece of tracing paper over my drawing and, using a technical drawing pen, I traced over the original design, refining and simplifying it as I went along.

As I was designing the stencil I was also keeping in mind the fact that the texture of the chair was fairly coarse and would not register delicate shapes.

If you have not altered your design radically during the course of the tracing you can use it to trace your design onto the plastic film. Otherwise you may like to make a second, cleaner tracing before you proceed.

I taped my tracing onto a flat work surface and then taped the plastic film over it, matt side uppermost. Using the same pen again and keeping the line as fine and as accurate as possible, I traced the design onto the film.

To cut the film I laid the plastic shiny-side up on my cutting mat. Using a *sharp* craft knife and cutting as evenly and accurately as possible, I began to cut out my stencil. I kept turning the stencil all the time to ensure that I always cut towards myself. When I had finished cutting I checked to make sure that I had no jagged edges and then tried the stencil out on a spare piece of paper to see if it needed any last-minute adjustments.

APPLYING THE PAINT

After checking the stencil, I measured the back of the chair and lightly marked the centre. I intended to use my stencil twice on the chair back – the right way round on one side of the mid-line and flipped over on the other.

As the back of the chair was curved it took quite a bit of masking tape to hold it in position. It is possible, and even advisable on some delicate surfaces, to use spray adhesives for holding stencils temporarily in position, but on a rough background like this one there is nothing quite like masking tape.

Once the stencil was firmly taped down, I poured a little of the acrylic craft paint into a saucer and took some of it up on the end of my stencil brush. I then pounced the brush onto a spare piece of paper until I had worked most of the paint off and was only making a slight impression.

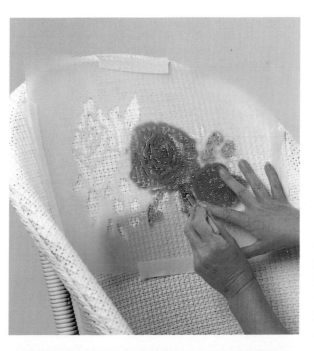

◄**Stencilling the chair**
I pounced the stencil brush through my stencil, using my other hand to hold the adjacent edges down as I worked.

◄**The revamped chair**
The stencil for this little bedroom chair was based on the fabric design of the seat, but had to be kept fairly simple because of the coarse nature of the wicker.

▶ Tacking on the fabric
If you use a proper upholstery hammer it makes life a lot easier as one end is magnetic. This means you can have one hand free to pull the fabric while you hammer in the holding tacks with the other.

UPHOLSTERING THE CHAIR SEAT

The upholstered chair seat was covered in torn blue material but, when this was removed, it revealed the original fabric quite intact. In fact the only thing that was wrong with the seat was that it had developed a little hollow in the middle where the stuffing had disappeared.

I cut some small pieces of cotton felt wadding and laid these in the hollow until I had brought the seat up to one level and then I cut a bigger piece of the wadding to cover the seat entirely. I then cut a piece of the patterned fabric approximately 7.5cm (3in) larger all around than the seat to cover it. I proceeded to do this in a similar way to covering the ottoman, by stretching the fabric over the wadding and attaching it to the frame with tacks in the base of the frame (see page 73).

I then trimmed off the excess fabric and cut a piece of canvas 2cm (¾in) larger all around than the base of the seat. Turning this allowance under, I tacked the canvas onto the bottom of the frame and replaced the newly padded seat back in the chair.

Then and only then did I begin to pounce the brush onto my stencil, using my free hand to hold the adjacent edges of the stencil down as I worked.

If you are like me, you will have childhood memories of being hardly able to wait until you could remove a stencil and reveal the results of an energetic stencilling session, only to be horribly disappointed by the smudges and runs when it was finally unveiled. It was quite a while before I eventually learned that the *less* paint you have on the brush, the better the stencil is likely to be. By building up the paint slowly, it is also possible to gradate the colour and achieve a sense of form in your stencils; I did this to the roses and leaves by using more than one shade of pink and green.

When I finished my first session of stencilling, I removed the stencil and washed off the paint with warm soapy water. I then dried it and taped it opposite the first stencil, in reverse. I completed the second side to match the first and also used part of the stencil to make a motif at the base of the chair.

Ottoman

Since I came into possession of mine, I am thinking of starting the Ottoman Appreciation Society. An ottoman really is one of the most versatile pieces of furniture.

Quite apart from its well-known storage potential it seems to have so many other functions. I use mine for hiding all manner of things from dubious telephone accounts to Christmas presents. I get dressed sitting on it, chuck clothes on it at night and even stand on it to change the light bulb.

I don't know how I ever managed without it!

MATERIALS
Oil-based white spray paint
Masking tape
Stencil (see page 70)
Stencil brush

Acrylic craft paints
Clear, satin polyurethane spray varnish
50cm (20in) thick polyester wadding
Scissors
50cm (20in) patterned fabric
10mm (⅜in) fine tacks
Small hammer
Glue gun or any strong colourless glue
Approximately 2·5m (8ft 4in) trimming

This ottoman is made from the same material as the little bedroom chair and therefore needed to be washed carefully before being given several thin layers of spray paint.

When the paint was dry I taped on the same stencil as I had used on the chair, adapting it to fit the shape and completing it in the same colours (see page 71), before finishing with spray varnish.

REPLACING THE SEAT FABRIC

The ottoman lid was covered in a very sorry-looking blue fabric and trimmed in gold plastic! I removed this and the original covering underneath to reveal some ancient, but still serviceable, wadding, which I covered with a piece of thick polyester wadding, to give the top a plumper and smoother surface.

Using the lid as a template, I cut out a piece of fabric which was the same shape but 7·5cm (3in) larger all around. I placed this piece of fabric over the new wadding and stood the lid on its front edge so that I could attach the cover to the back strut of the lid with three holding tacks. Pulling against these tacks, I then smoothed the fabric over the lid and fixed the front in place in a similar way.

Having put a holding tack in each side, I then worked my way around the lid, gently shaping the rounded front corners with tiny pleats and trimming of the excess fabric when I had finished.

Finally, using a glue gun, I glued on the braid trimming so that it covered the tacks completely.

◀ **The ottoman**
The previous owner of this ottoman must have had a taste for the exotic. The gold plastic trim around the edge was still blinding even though the rest of it had become terribly faded and scuffed.

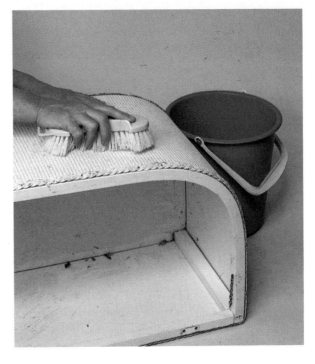

◀ **Scrubbing the weave**
The weave on the ottoman was surprisingly free of paint but very dusty. I gave it a quick scrub with warm soapy water, trying to work fast and drying it quickly as I went so that the water did not soak into the weave which is made from rolled paper.

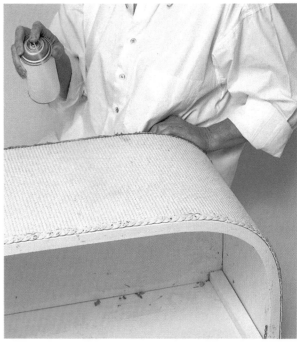

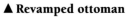
▲ Revamped ottoman
The stencilled design on the ottoman was made by adapting the original bedroom chair stencil in various ways, including using it in reverse.

▶ Spraying the ottoman
When the ottoman was clean and dry, I gave it several thin coats of oil-based spray paint, making sure before I applied each coat, that the previous layer was dry.

▶ Gluing on the trim
I used a glue gun to attach the trim – it is certainly the easiest way of doing it. If you don't own a glue gun, any quick-drying transparent glue will do.

Dressing Table

I had been longing for a kidney-shaped dressing table for absolutely ages when I finally saw this one at a junk market. It was on a stall piled high with a lot of fashionable old pine and the stallholder looked as if he would charge way over the odds and be a hard nut to crack. I had to formulate a plan.

I wanted the dressing table so much that I had to walk up and down, rehearsing my bartering technique, for some time, before I felt sufficiently psyched-up to ask him the price.

When I eventually did, in a rather bored, disinterested way, and he answered me with an unexpectedly low single figure, I immediately assumed it was his abbreviated, trader's way of saying hundreds and walked away, feeling utterly miserable.

I was halfway round the market before it dawned on me what he'd really meant, so I promtly ran back to the stall at full speed. I was so out of breath when I arrived that I dismissed all thoughts of bargaining and paid him the asking price out of sheer relief!

MATERIALS
Fine and super-fine sandpaper
Tack rag
Primer
White eggshell paint
White spirit
2 x 4cm (1½in) house-painting brushes
Artist's oil colours: Rose Madder, Cadmium Yellow, Raw Umber
Transparent oil glaze
3 small, non-plastic containers
Old tablespoon
Lint-free rag
Artist's paintbrush (sable or synthetic mixture)
Badger softener
Clear, satin polyurethane varnish
Clean rag

Before I did anything else I took my prize to the strippers to remove the thick layers of white paint which seemed to have been put on in great haste.

When the dressing table returned the mirror frames had been reduced to a bundle of sticks and I realized that the paint had been all that had held them together. Luckily the 'sticks' of moulding were still in good condition, so I took them to the picture framer and had the corners repinned. He did them with a power hammer in minutes and charged so little that it wasn't worth doing it myself.

I rubbed the rest of the dressing table down with fine sandpaper and tried to get the surface as smooth as possible as I had decided to marble it.

I went over it carefully with the tack rag and then gave it a coat of white primer which I left to dry for the recommended time.

I lightly rubbed down the primer with the fine sandpaper and then tacked the surface again before giving it a coat of eggshell paint, slightly thinned down with white spirit.

If you thin down the paint you will probably need to give the piece at least one extra coat of paint, but you will get a much smoother surface as a result.

I gave the dressing table four coats of paint and left each layer to dry for 24 hours. Between applications, I rubbed down the dry paint with super-fine sandpaper and dusted it with the tack rag before painting on the next coat.

As the drawers and main body of the dressing table were going to be concealed beneath curtains, I must admit that I abandoned them at this point and directed all my attention to the top of the dressing table and the frames of the mirrors.

MARBLING THE DRESSING TABLE
Working with a small piece of the curtain fabric beside me and using oil paints and white eggshell paint, I mixed up two pinks to match the pinks of the roses and one a little darker which I intended to use for the veins in the marble:

▲ **The dressing table**
I consider this dressing table to be one of my major bargains even though the mirror frames did fall apart at the strippers!

▶ Ragging the glaze
While the glaze was still wet, I took a piece of lint-free rag and, making it into a crumpled wad, I pressed it firmly and quickly all over the glazed area.

▶ Applying the veins
To give the veins a more natural look, hold the paintbrush loosely at one end rather than grabbing it fiercely by the ferrule.

First pink
2·5cm (1in) Rose Madder + small squeeze of Cadmium Yellow + smaller squeeze of Raw Umber + a little white eggshell + 3 tablespoons each of white spirit and transparent oil glaze

Second pink
2·5cm (1in) Rose Madder + very small squeeze of Raw Umber + a little white eggshell + 3 tablespoons each of white spirit and transparent oil glaze

Darker pink for veining
Rose Madder + Raw Umber + small touch of white eggshell + a little white spirit

I mixed each of the first two sets of colours in separate small containers and dissolved them thoroughly with enough of the white spirit to make them creamy. I then gradually added the transparent oil glaze and stirred that well into the mixture, using an old tablespoon. Finally I stirred in the rest of the white spirit.

This mixture should be quite fluid and look transparent when brushed out experimentally onto a piece of white paper. It should not be so thin, however, that it does not hold its shape when you attempt to rag it later.

I took the first of the pink glazes and painted irregular patches of glaze all over the top of the dressing table.

I then partially filled in the open areas with similar patches of the second glaze, but left some of the white base coat showing as a third colour.

While the glaze was still wet, I took a piece of lint-free rag and, making it into a crumpled wad, I pressed it firmly and quickly all over the glazed area. This gave a subtle, loose texture to the glaze which made a perfect background for the marble.

Taking the third mixture and an artist's paintbrush, I then began to paint on the veining. Although this is faux marble and is not seriously trying to imitate natural marble, it will look more realistic if you ensure that the veining lines travel diagonally and either begin and finish on the edge of the piece or when they connect up with another vein. Real veins do not appear out of nowhere!

◀ **Softening the veins**
Using a badger softener, I lightly dusted the veins along their length in a diagonal direction. I repeated this in both directions and then very lightly across the lines from side to side.

◀ **Pinning heading tape**
I pinned the Velcro heading tape over the turn-in and machined it in place, pulling the strings free and turning the heading under neatly at each end.

The veins will also have a more natural and random quality if you hold the paintbrush loosely at one end rather than grabbing it fiercely by the ferrule.

When I had completed the veining I took my badger softener and began lightly dusting the veins along their length in a diagonal direction. I did this in both directions and then repeated the dusting very lightly across the lines from side to side. Badger softeners do give you the most incredibly soft finish, but they are expensive. Cheaper alternatives you might like to experiment with are a dusting brush, an old badger shaving brush or even a soft cosmetic 'blusher' brush.

I left the faux marbling to dry for 24 hours and then gave it a coat of clear, satin polyurethane varnish.

The mirror frames had already had several layers of thin white eggshell and I now painted them with irregular patches of the first two glazes. After allowing the glazes to settle for a few minutes, I dabbed the surface firmly with a clean rag so that the glazes were left mainly in the moulding.

I then varnished the frames as before and replaced the glass which had been removed before the stripping.

Dressing Table Curtains

MATERIALS
Tape measure
Scissors
3m (10ft) patterned fabric, 135cm (54in) wide
4m (4½yd) No.3 piping cord
1m (3ft 4in) plain fabric, 135cm (54in) wide
4m (4½yd) curtain heading
4m (4½yd) Velcro heading tape
2m (2¼yd) Velcro
Cotton
Pins

The dressing table already had runners for a curtain underneath the now-marbled top and I decided to make a pair of curtains with a piped frill to hang from these runners.

I also planned a second frill to hang over the top of the curtain which would be attached to the edge of the dressing table-top with Velcro.

MEASURING & CUTTING OUT CURTAINS

I measured the height of the dressing table from the floor to the runners and the length of each runner. I wanted the curtains to be quite full and gathered and so I multiplied the length of each runner by two to arrive at the required width of the curtains.

Then, allowing for a 10cm (4in) frill at the bottom and two 12mm (½in) seam allowances, I worked out the depth of each curtain and then cut them out of the patterned fabric.

I cut out several strips of the same fabric for the bottom frills and machined them together until I had two long strips, which were each twice the width of a curtain and 12·5cm (5in) long. This allowed for the hem and a 12mm (½in) seam allowance.

I measured around the edge of the curved dressing table-top and doubled this measurement to arrive at the length of the top frill. I intended this to be 15cm (6in) deep and I added on 2·5cm (1in) for two 12mm (½in) seam allowances. I cut out several strips of patterned fabric for this frill and machined the strips together as I had done for the bottom frill.

I then covered two lengths of piping cord, each one the width of one curtain, with the plain fabric (see page 91). I machined the covered cord to the bottoms of the curtains (see page 91) before hemming both sides.

I then completed the hemming by trimming the cord and tucking in the remains of the plain fabric at either end.

I gathered and hemmed both the bottom frills (see page 91) and attached them to the bottoms of the curtains by placing right sides and raw edges together and machining as close to the piping as possible.

I then folded in 12mm (½in) along the top of each curtain and machined the curtain heading in place, pulling free the strings and tucking the heading under neatly at both ends.

It then only remained to pull up the strings to the required length and put in some curtain hooks so that I could then hang the curtains from the runners on the dressing table.

ADDING THE TOP FRILL

To complete the top frill, I cut several 5cm (2in) strips on the cross from the plain fabric. I then joined these strips together to make one long strip, which was the same length as the top frill (see page 91). This was the binding. I folded this in half lengthwise, and pressed it in place with the iron. I then folded both long edges into the middle and pressed it again.

I placed this binding along the length of the top frill so that both right sides were together and one raw edge of the binding was against the raw edge of the frill. I then machined the two pieces together along the unfolded crease in the binding.

I trimmed the excess material from the seam and folded the binding back so that the other creased edge was on the wrong side of the fabric and against the row of machine stitches. I neatly hemmed the binding along this edge, picking up every second or third stitch without going through the fabric.

I hemmed both ends of the frill and pressed the binding and a 12mm (½in) turn-in along the other edge. I then pinned the Velcro heading tape over the turn-in and machined it in place, pulling the strings free and turning the heading under neatly at either end.

Finally, I peeled the protective covering from the back of the Velcro and stuck it all around the edge of the top of the dressing table. I pulled up the strings on the frill until it was the right length and pressed the Velcro heading against the strip where it held quite firmly.

As I still had a little of the main fabric left over, I also made a little bow for the middle of the top frill (see page 91), which I fixed in place with a couple of stitches.

The Bathroom

Most of us do not have very big bathrooms and should therefore not go in for anything too hectic in the way of decoration. I have used the soft turquoise of a

verdigris finish on the metal handle and mirror and picked up a similar colour on the wicker with just a splash of gold for glamour!

Bathrooms are often the most eccentric, flamboyant or entertaining rooms in the house. For some unknown reason even those people who conform rigidly to the norm in every other room in the home, have been known to express their individuality quite forcefully when it comes to bathroom decor.

If you are new to the pastime of junk recycling, the bathroom is certainly one of the best places to start your career, if you wish to avoid the comments of startled friends and family alike.

No one will give it a second thought if you smother everything in the bathroom with sea-shells and a verdigris finish, but they may need time to get used to the idea elsewhere in the house.

▲ The linen basket
The linen basket was bashed about a bit, but there was nothing that a coat or two of spray paint wouldn't cover.

Wicker Linen Basket

This wicker linen basket was bought at a garage sale under dream conditions. It was pouring with rain and the house in question was only just down the road from where I live.

The people who lived there were obviously not well versed in holding garage sales and had only put up one sign advertising the sale, the night before, on a tree outside the house.

This meant that customers were going to be restricted to local, dog walking, garage-sale fanatics who didn't mind the rain, or to those car drivers who could read dripping, red felt pen notices at speed.

Needless to say, Rover and I had the field to ourselves and came away with some really wonderful bargains, including this wicker linen basket and a tartan all-weather dog coat.

MATERIALS
White oil-based spray paint
Scissors
1m (40in) curtain lining, 1·2m (48in) wide
PVA glue
Bowl
Dressmaker's pins
Old plastic bags
Natural sponge
Acrylic craft paint
Gold bronzing powder
Acrylic varnish
Clear polyurethane varnish

This linen basket is made with the same mysterious wicker as the bedroom chair and ottoman (see page 70) but, luckily, has managed to survive without getting its weave clogged up.

It was rather dirty, though, and I scrubbed it thoroughly with warm soapy water, before allowing it to dry; then I gave the basket several thin coats of spray paint, allowing it to dry between each coat.

MAKING THE SWAG & BOW
I cut out several strips of curtain lining to make the swag and bow:

Swag:
1 piece measuring 1·2m x 30cm (48in x 12in)
Bow:
1 piece measuring 25cm x 30cm (10in x 12in)
Tails:
2 pieces each measuring 25cm x 25cm (10in x 10in)
Knot:
1 piece measuring 15cm x 12·5cm (6in x 5in)

I diluted some of the PVA glue in a bowl (1 part PVA to 2 parts water) to act as a stiffener. Taking the strip of fabric cut for the swag, I soaked it in the stiffener and then laid it out lengthwise on a clean work surface. I then turned in the raw edges along both long sides, and, gathering up an end in each hand, I pulled the swag straight so that it fell into natural pleats.

Still holding both ends, I draped the swag around the middle of the linen basket with the folded-in raw edges facing inwards. Holding the ends of the swag at the front of the linen basket, I pulled hard until the pleated swag was touching the linen basket all around.

I overlapped the swag slightly at the front of the basket and, after checking that it was lying straight and symmetrically all around the basket, I trimmed off the excess fabric. Then I laid the basket on its back with a clean, plastic bag under the swag. (If the swag slips a little, hold it in place temporarily with some dressmaker's pins.)

Next, I soaked the tail pieces in the glue mix and then smoothed them out flat on the work surface. Taking them separately, I turned each long side in towards the middle so that they overlapped slightly and then trimmed one end of each tail diagonally. I cut a notch out of the remaining two ends, as you might do a piece of ribbon.

Placing the two diagonal ends together, like an arrowhead, I laid the wet tails over the join of the swag with

◄ Arranging the swag
I draped the wet swag around the linen basket and pulled the ends tight, so that the fabric was pressed against all the sides. I then crossed over the ends and laid the basket on its back before cutting off the excess.

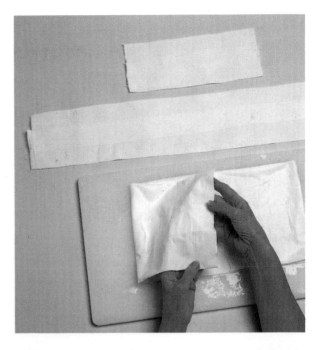

► Folding the bow fabric
I smoothed out the pieces of fabric for the bow and tails and folded both sides lengthwise into the middle on each piece. I then took the piece intended for the bow and folded both ends into the middle.

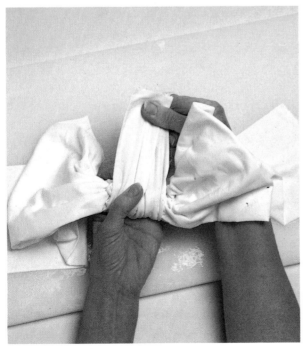

◄ Making the 'knot'
I took the short piece of fabric intended for the 'knot' and wound it tightly around the middle of the bow so that it covered the place where the two loops met and ended at the back of the bow.

► Stuffing the bow
When the bow was in place on the swag, I stuffed each loop with some crumpled pieces of plastic bag to give the fabric some shape.

▶ Painting the bow

As the weave was already too clogged up to strip, I painted the wastepaper basket and bow with eggshell paint, using a paintbrush instead of a spray paint.

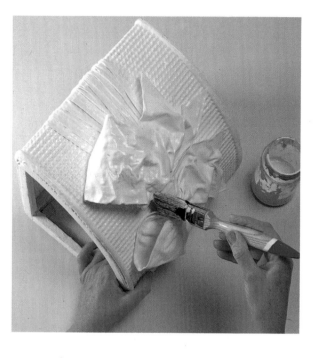

▶ Sponging

When the paint was completely dry, I sponged on some diluted acrylic paint. Always test the sponging several times on a spare piece of paper until all the excess paint is gone and you are left with a clear impression of the texture.

their seams at the back and arranged them flat on the basket with just a little artistic wrinkle here and there.

I put the remaining pieces of fabric in the stiffener and laid them out flat and folded them as I had the tails. Taking the largest strip, I turned both ends into the middle to form a bow and overlapped them a little. I then wound the smaller strip around the middle so that it was slightly gathered and started and finished over the join.

Turning the bow over so that all the joins were at the back, I laid it over the join in the swag and on top of the tails. I then arranged the bow so that the swag join and the un-notched tail ends were well hidden, before stuffing the loops of the bow with some crumpled pieces of plastic bag to hold them open while they were drying.

When you stuff a bow, don't use too many pieces of plastic bag or the bows will look too stiff. I even scrunch the fabric up a bit so that the loops look more natural. I also try to make sure that the maximum amount of bow fabric is touching the linen basket so that it is well glued on when it dries.

When the fabric had thoroughly dried out, I gave it several coats of spray paint until it had a similar finish to the basket.

Finally, I sponged the basket with some thinned acrylic paint (see page 21) and then with some gold bronzing powder, mixed into some acrylic varnish.

Items such as this linen basket don't normally need to be varnished, especially as the varnish is bound to yellow the pastel colours slightly, but if you really must, use either clear satin or gloss polyurethane varnish.

WASTEPAPER BASKET

The little wastepaper basket was decorated in exactly the same way as the linen basket except that because the weave was already clogged up beyond redemption, I brushed on white eggshell paint instead of spraying it on.

If you do have some of either this weave or Lloyd Loom which is only a little clogged or badly painted, the 'cold chemical' non-caustic method of professional stripping will get rid of it for you.

▲ The revamped basket
Let yourself go when arranging giant swags and bows on linen baskets. They look much more interesting and flamboyant if you leave them slightly crumpled and squashed.

Wall Mirror

Believe it or not, I didn't take any trips to the seaside to collect all the shells for this mirror. Most of them came from charity shops and junk fairs with just one small bag of very pretty ones from a florist.

You do need a great many similar shells to cover a frame successfully, especially if you want it to be symmetrical. I found that shell flowerpot hangers and necklaces turn up very often on junk stalls and the little shells from them, when they are unthreaded, are very useful for filling in the spaces. If you are not a beachcomber though and don't find anyone selling their collection at a junk fair, there are still some shops around that specialize in shells, as well as florists that sell them for flower arranging and other forms of decoration.

MATERIALS
Drawing paper & pencil
Shells
Ruler
Chalk
Glue gun or other quick-setting glue
Clear, gloss polyurethane varnish
Small, stiff brush
Small piece of card with semi-circle cut out of one side

Luckily, I had found a mirror with a flat frame, which is fairly essential for this project, but which was surprisingly hard to find when I was actually looking for one!

First I laid the mirror on the sheet of paper and drew around the outside of it. Then, measuring the width of the frame, I drew another rectangle inside the first so that I had the dimensions of the frame on paper.

I placed the paper on a tray which was a little larger than the frame, and began to arrange and re-arrange my shells on the drawn frame until I came up with a design I liked.

The reason for using the tray was to avoid spilling the shells as I moved the paper around. If you do not possess a large enough tray or similar item, lay the paper on a surface where it is not likely to be disturbed for a while.

As I was working, I put several small shells to one side so that I could use them later to decorate the sides of the frame, which were not shown on the drawing.

The design will look more attractive if you have at least one point of interest where you have grouped larger and more colourful shells. In my design I have a large group at the top and a smaller one at the bottom, but I have also given some extra attention to the corners.

I measured along the top and bottom edges of my

◀ **Arranging the shells**
I drew the frame to scale on paper and laid this on a tray. Then I arranged the shells until I had a pleasing, well-balanced design.

◀ **Gluing on the shells**
Most strong glues will hold the shells in place, but make sure you use one which only needs a single application and which dries transparently. If you use a glue gun, be careful that you do not burn your fingers.

▶ **Varnishing the shells**
When varnishing the shells, mask the mirror glass with a piece of card. You may need to cut a curve into the side of the card so that it fits around the shells.

▶ **The revamped mirror**
Make sure that you use a strong picture hook before attempting to hang one of these shell mirrors. The combination of mirror, frame and shells make this a very weighty item!

actual frame and marked the centres with chalk to make sure that my large groups of shells didn't end up lopsided.

Then, starting with the large groups, I began to transfer the shells from the paper frame to the real one, gluing each one into place with the glue gun. After completing the main areas, I used many of the little shells, which I had saved earlier, to decorate the sides.

When the frame was completely covered and the glue was dry, I gave the shells two coats of varnish using a small, stiff brush. To ensure that the varnish did not touch the glass, I used the shaped card as a shield. I left the frame to dry for 24 hours between applications.

The varnish brings up all the beautiful colours in the shells and they look as if they have just been washed by the sea.

Metal Mirror & Door Handles

These days, we seem to have an obsession for making things look worn and neglected. We can't wait to make objects look rusty, crazed, fly-blown, distressed or just plain dusty. Of all the antiquing techniques, however, I think my favourite is verdigris, which, of course, is the effect you get when certain metals, such as copper and brass, are left to their own devices and become discoloured and corroded with age.

MATERIALS
Masking tape
Jam jars
4cm (1½in) house-painting brush
Old tablespoon
Emulsion paint: Dark Blue-green, Peppermint Green, Pale Blue, Pale Turquoise
Methylated spirits
Sieve
Whiting
Several hog's-hair artist's paintbrushes
Cloth
PVA glue

You may have trouble getting hold of the Dark Green emulsion in a small size but, if you are working on a small item, you will probably find that the little trial pots of emulsion – which most paint manufacturers produce nowadays – will give you plenty of paint.

Before I did anything else I washed all the metal in hot, soapy water to get rid of any dust and grease and then dried everything thoroughly. I also masked off the mirror with some masking tape and made up half a jam jar of diluted, Dark Green emulsion paint (1 part emulsion paint to 3 parts water). Then I painted the diluted emulsion onto the mirror frame and stand as well as the door plates and knobs and left them to dry.

VERDIGRIS PAINT TECHNIQUE

To make up the verdigris pastes, I put a tablespoonful of each of the pastel emulsion paints into separate jam jars and stirred two tablespoonfuls of methylated spirits into each colour. To each of these I added enough sieved whiting to make a firm mixture.

Working on the mirror only and using a hog's-hair brush I went over all the frame and stand using all three colours and trying to make the distribution of colour and texture as random as possible.

When the verdigris pastes had dried out, which did not take very long, I went over the mirror again, lightly dabbing it all over with water on a clean brush.

While the frame was still damp I sprinkled on some more sieved whiting and dabbed and pushed this into the moulding of the frame with my fingers. I also took a little of the diluted base green and trickled a very small amount here and there, but be careful not to overdo this as it could spoil the effect.

As the frame began to dry out again I went over it with a dry cloth, rubbing some of it back to the green base coat and a very little of the raised areas back to the metal. Most of it I left untouched. While the frame was drying, I gave the finger plates and door knobs the same treatment.

When they were all quite dry I sealed them with a coat of diluted PVA glue (2 parts water to 1 part PVA).

▲▼**Mirror & door handles**
The metal was definitely not worth cleaning up, but it was very decorative in both cases and ideal for a verdigris finish.

◀ Mixing the pastes
To make up the verdigris pastes, I put a tablespoonful of each of the pastel emulsion paints into separate jam jars and stirred 2 tablespoonfuls of methylated spirits into each colour.

◀ Dabbing on whiting
When the verdigris pastes had dried out, I went over the work again, dabbing it all over with water on a clean brush. I then sprinkled on some more sieved whiting and dabbed and pushed this into the moulding with my fingers.

▶ The revamped mirror
As well as a verdigris finish being wonderful for covering up metals which have become dull and worn, it is also a very accommodating and lovely colour which will go with almost anything.

The Conservatory

As these chairs had such a curly design and the table had so many slats, I saved myself hours of work by using spray paint. It did cost a little more, but as the table was a skip victim and the chairs were a bargain, I felt justified.

If there is one thing that you would never have any trouble furnishing from a junk market, it is a conservatory. If I had bought everything about which I had said 'that would look nice in the conservatory', there would definitely not be any space left for me, let alone anyone else.

It is only my iron will which has restricted the chairs *alone* to those that go with the table and two or three more for lounging. I nearly had a wicker emperor's chair, something called a butterfly throne, several delightful wicker settees, numerous old Lloyd Looms in various stages of tattiness *and* their accompanying tables, footstools, etc . . . and that's not counting the jardinières, window boxes, bamboo blinds, plant stands, pots and parrot cages . . . so do be careful!

▶ **The table and chairs**
Because this table and chairs are going to spend the best part of their lives out in the elements they will have to be treated for rust and then painted with specially protective paint.

▶ **Rubbing down**
The weather and stripping had lifted the grain on the table-top and it needed rubbing down, first with medium grade and then with fine sandpaper.

Garden Table & Chairs

These chairs were originally white and belonged to a lady who loved to contemplate their pretty wrought iron shapes as they stood on her patio, but who just hated the impression they quite literally made on her, a few minutes after sitting in them!

Luckily the cushion solution never occurred to her and, after a summer of intense discomfort, she was happy to sell them to me for the proverbial song.

The table was even cheaper as it was 'rescued' from a roadside skip one cold and frosty morning.

REVAMPING THE GARDEN TABLE

MATERIALS
Fine wire wool
Rust remover
Paint stripper
Stripping tool
Medium and fine sandpaper
Tack rag
Wood primer
4cm (1½in) house-painting brush
3 spray tins of green anti-corrosive paint (eg Hammerite)

The garden table was partly metal and partly wood, but luckily good old Hammerite could handle both or I should have had the problem of trying to match the paints.

The metal legs were in fairly good condition, apart from a little rust, so I decided to remove the screws that held the legs on and give them a good wash in hot, soapy water. Using the wire wool, I rubbed off any loose paintwork which came to light, and made a note of the inevitable rust spots.

When the legs had dried, I treated the rust spots with the rust remover and wire wool until the bare metal was gleaming. Rust removers are so good nowadays that this procedure usually takes a few minutes, but if the thought of it still appals you, it is usually alright if all you do is rub off any *loose* rust with sandpaper.

This left me with the problem of the table-top which definitely needed stripping and which I decided to do by hand (see page 20). As the table-top had taken such a beating, first by the elements and then by the stripping, my next job was to rub it down first with some medium grade and then with some fine sandpaper. I then went over it with a tack rag (see page 13) and primed it, painting as smoothly as possible and taking care to keep the brush strokes going in the same direction as the grain.

When the primer had dried I rubbed it down lightly once more, tacked it and gave it four or five applications of spray Hammerite (see page 16). Finally, when everything was dry, I re-united the table with its smart new legs.

MAKING THE TABLECLOTH

MATERIALS
1·5m (62in) PVC fabric, 1·3m (52in) wide
Scissors
Pencil
String
Drawing pin
4·5m (8½ft) fringing
Cotton

Placing the fabric flat on the floor, I folded one corner over to its opposite side so that the width was lying against the length. This formed a triangle of double material with a strip of single material left over, which I trimmed off. I folded the material in two again so that I now had a narrower triangle made from four layers of material.

I tied one end of a length of string to my pencil and made a loop at the other end so that I could fix it to the floor with a drawing pin at the apex of the triangle. I adjusted the string so that the pencil just reached the farthest side of the triangle. Then, keeping the string taut, I drew a curved line across this side of fabric.

I carefully cut along this curve through the four layers of fabric so that, when I opened the whole thing up, hey presto! – I had a circular tablecloth.

I basted the fringe around the edge of the cloth, making a neat join by tucking one end over the other. Remembering to change my sewing machine needle to one which was suited to the more solid fabric, I finally machined the fringe in place.

REVAMPING THE CHAIRS

MATERIALS
Fine wire wool (000 gauge)
Rust remover
Green anti-corrosive spray paint (eg Hammerite, approximately 1 tin per chair)
Old newspapers
Scissors
Ruler
Approximately 2·5m (8ft 4in) main fabric
3·5m (11ft 10in) piping cord
2m (2¼yd) plain fabric
2 cushion pads, 40cm x 40cm (16in x 16in)
2 cushion pads, 30cm x 30cm (12in x 12in)
Cotton
Needles
Pins

My chairs had been standing out in the garden and were rain-splashed and generally quite mucky, so I treated them in exactly the same way as I had the table legs (see page 88).

Once the rust had been treated, I was able to begin painting. I had opted to use the same spray paint because of the curly nature of the wrought ironwork and I began by turning the chairs upside down and spraying all the surfaces I could see from that angle. I then turned them the right way up and repeated the process. When I had done this three or four times I had two shiny, new chairs just waiting to have their cushions made.

A word of caution regarding spray paints, especially if you have had little or no experience of them: do follow the instructions carefully and don't attempt to put too much

▶ Marking the circle
Keeping the string as taut as possible, I drew a curved line at the base of the fabric triangle to mark out the circle.

▶ Spraying the chair
It is better to spray on several thin layers of paint as the paint will run and drip if you spray on too much at a time.

paint on at any one time or you will get runs or drips. Even so, with this type of paint the *layers* do have to be built up in fairly quick succession so that they can meld together before the paint begins to 'cure'.

Another thing to remember is that spray paint can travel further than the item you are painting; although I deliberately chose a wind-free day to paint my chairs, and stood them outside on acres of newspaper, I still ended up with green sandals and decidedly gangrenous-looking feet – so take care!

MAKING THE CUSHIONS

Before I started cutting out the cushions I made myself some very simple paper patterns out of newspaper.

I cut out one square measuring 35cm x 35cm (14in x 14in) for the smaller cushion and one measuring 45cm x 45cm (18in x 18in) for the larger one.

To make the paper pattern for the seat cushion's ties, I drew a line 70cm (28in) long on a piece of paper and then drew a 6cm (2½in) line at right angles to the top of it and a 10cm (4in) line at right angles to the bottom. By joining the ends of these short lines, I made a wedge shape with three straight sides and one that sloped diagonally.

Working at the broad end of the wedge, I measured 14cm (5½in) up the sloping side and marked it off. I then drew a curve from this mark to the corner where the straight side met the 10cm (4in) line.

When I cut out this pattern piece, I discarded the squared end at the bottom of the wedge and cut around the curve.

If you have as large a fabric design as I have, it looks attractive if you can arrange your pattern pieces so that you get a well-balanced section of the design in the centre of each cushion. This may only be possible on the front of each cushion, but if you cut out each side individually you may be able to achieve a good design on every side.

Plan your cutting strategy well before you start to wield your scissors, as you will need four of the ties and they really should be cut on double fabric with the straight side of the pattern placed on a fold.

MAKING THE PIPING & TIES

Each of my large cushions needed approximately 1·7m (5ft 8in) of piping cord and a similar amount of plain fabric to cover it. The fabric needed to be cut on the bias in strips approximately 4cm (1½in) wide and joined where necessary with 6mm (¼in) seams.

I covered the cord by laying it on the wrong side of the strip before folding the fabric evenly around it. I then pinned the fabric in place prior to basting it. Using the piping attachment on my machine so that I could get as close to the cord as possible, I machined the cord in place.

I folded the cut-out ties so that the right sides were facing and machined the raw edges together along the length and around the curve. I then turned them the right way out and pressed them flat so that the seam was along the edge.

MAKING THE SEAT CUSHIONS

I took half of the covered piping and pinned it to the right side of one of the larger cushion pieces so that the raw edges of the piping and cushion fabric were together.

I joined the piping cord by first cutting each side so that the strands of the cord were a slightly different length, and then twisting the two ends together so that they intermingled smoothly. I then joined the covering fabric by overlapping one side over the other and folding under the upper edge. Then I basted and machined the piping onto the cushion fabric.

Before attaching the other side of the cushion I notched the seam allowance on the piping cord at each corner. I arranged the ties so that they lay on the cushion with their raw edges pointing in the same direction as the cushion's raw edges. They were then pinned in pairs on either side of the two corners at the back of the cushion so that the straight edges were nearest the corners and about 2·5cm (1in) away from them. Then I basted them in place.

I then placed the other side of the cushion on top of the first so that both the right sides were together. Then I pinned, basted and machined it in place, so that the ties were machined in position, but leaving open the space between the back ones. Finally I trimmed off any excess

seam allowance and turned the cushion the right way out.

I pressed the cushion and filled it with one of the 40cm (16in) pads. I then turned in the remaining raw edges and slip-stitched them together.

MAKING THE FRILL

To make a nice, full frill I allowed twice as much fabric in the frill as there was in the cushion on each side. For example on the 30cm (12in) square cushions, I allowed 60cm (24in) of frill fabric for each side, making 2·4m (2¾yd) for the whole cushion.

I cut the fabric into 7·5cm (3in) wide strips and joined them together with 6mm (¼in) french seams where necessary. I then hemmed the whole length of the frill with a 6mm (¼in) hem.

My next job was to gather the frill and, using the gathering facility on my sewing machine, it did not take long to put a double row of gathering stitches close to the raw edge of the strip. If you are going to do this job by hand, however, I find that it is easiest if you thread the loose end of a reel of cotton and put one row of small basting stitches in and carefully gather these up.

MAKING THE FRILLED CUSHION

Having pulled up the gathering stitches so that the frill was the approximate size to go all around the cushion, I arranged the gathers so that they were evenly distributed along the length. Then I pinned the frill around the edge of one side of the cushion, with the right sides of the frill and the cushion together, and the raw edges together. I then joined the ends of the frill together with a french seam and basted and machined the frill in place, taking care to keep the gathers straight so that they did not get caught up in the machining at an angle.

I pinned the other side of the cushion to the first, with right sides together, and basted and machined the two halves together, leaving one side mostly open.

After turning the cushion the right way out and pressing it, I stuffed it with one of the 30cm (12in) pads and turned in and slip-stitched the raw edges together.

▲ **Attaching the piping**
With the raw edges together, I pinned the piping to the right side of the cushion fabric.

▲ The deck chair
There was something rather jaunty about this deck chair, in spite of its drab condition and I couldn't wait to restore it with colours more in keeping with its personality.

▶ Cutting out the hood
I carefully unpicked the old hood and used the pieces as patterns for the new one.

▶ Tacking on the canvas
When the second coat of varnish was dry, I tacked the seat canvas onto the frame with some round-headed tacks.

Deck Chair

The most intriguing thing about this deck chair is that on the very day when I first went looking for one *exactly* like it, I actually found it!

I was so amazed that I bought it, even though, in its hey-day, you could have kitted out a seaside promenade with deck chairs for the same price.

MATERIALS
4m (4½yd) deck chair canvas
Pins
Strong cotton
Fine sandpaper
Tack rag
Clear, matt polyurethane varnish
Jam jar
Tube of universal stainers (blue)
4cm (1½in) house-painting brush
Round-headed tacks
Glue gun or any strong, colourless glue
2m (2¼yd) cotton tassels

REPLACING THE CANVAS
When I went out to buy the deck chair canvas, I thought that there would only be a choice between stripes or plain material, but I was mistaken and came back with this gorgeous bright tartan.

Unfortunately I broke a cardinal rule and forgot to measure up before I went shopping. I had to rely on the advice of the man in the store who, although he was about the same vintage as the deck chair, got it wrong. This meant that some months later when I was actually doing the job and needed some more fabric, there was none left in the stores. After telephoning all the big stores without any luck, I eventually found some in the last place I thought of looking . . . my local shop. But be warned, you might not be so lucky!

Before I could do anything else to the deck chair, I had to take off all the existing canvas carefully so that I could

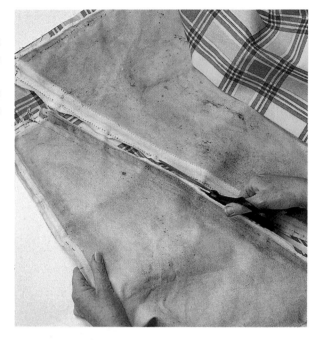

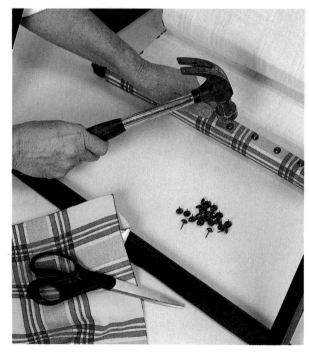

use the pieces as patterns for the new material. The hood in particular had to be unstitched and pressed flat. I was surprised to find that even the seemingly straight up and down seat had been carefully folded so that it tapered towards the front.

Having noted all the pattern details as I took the canvas apart, I pinned the old canvas to the new and cut out the pattern pieces.

Then, making sure that I remembered to change the needle in the sewing machine for one that would stitch through canvas, it was relatively simple to re-assemble the hood and press in the folds on the front of the seat.

DOING UP THE FRAME

The frame meanwhile needed to have the dirt of ages literally scrubbed off it. When it was dry I rubbed it down with some fine sandpaper and then went over it with the tack rag (see page 13).

I wanted to varnish the frame against the weather and I decided to tint the varnish blue so that the frame would pick up the background colour of the tartan canvas.

I decanted some of the varnish into a jam jar and added a generous squeeze of universal stainers which I mixed in well. I then gave the frame two coats of the blue varnish, leaving 24 hours' drying time after each application.

When the second coat was dry I tacked the seat canvas onto the frame with some round-headed tacks and fixed the hood on with a tack in each corner. Finally, using my glue gun (or any strong glue that dries transparently will do), I fixed the brilliant yellow tassels around the edge of the hood.

The deck chair was a great success with fair-skinned friends and family alike. I'm looking for its twin with a footstool now.

Index

Suppliers

Creative Interiors
20 Station Parade, Chipstead, Surrey CR5 3TE
Telephone 0737 555443

With many thanks to Carol Good for her invaluable advice, particularly on the subject of loose covers!

Traditions
Traditional Furnishings and Upholstery,
259 Ewell Road, Surbiton, Surrey KT6 7AA
Telephone 081–390 4472

This shop is run by Jane McDonald and Linda Flannery, who I would like to thank for giving me so much good and friendly advice.

Southside Strippers
Unit 9, Glenville Mews, Kimber Road, Wandsworth, London SW18 4NJ
Telephone 081–875 0866

John at Southside Strippers uses the 'cold chemical' method of stripping and will strip all types of wood including delicate veneers, gesso work and the dreaded Lloyd Loom! I wouldn't go anywhere else.

C. Brewers and Sons Ltd
86–88 Ewell Road, Surbiton, Surrey KT6 6EX
Telephone 081–399 1054

Specialist suppliers of decorating materials.
There are several Brewers dotted around, but I would like to thank the staff at Surbiton for being especially friendly and helpful . . . even when I go in just as they are closing!

Romo Fabrics
Lowmoor Road, Kirkby-in-Ashfield,
Nottinghamshire NG17 7DE
Telephone 0623 750005

Suppliers of fabrics.

Arthur Sanderson and Sons Ltd
6 Cavendish Square, London W1M 9HA
Telephone 071–636 7800

Suppliers of paint and fabric.

John Myland Ltd
80 Norwood High Street, London SE27 9N
Telephone 081–761 570

Manufacturers and suppliers of wood finish products and specialist paint products